W9-CAX-635

HOW A CHILDHOOD WAS STOLEN AND A TRUST BETRAYED

The Little Prisoner

JANE ELLIOTT

with Andrew Crofts

HarperElement
An Imprint of HarperCollins*Publishers*
77–85 Fulham Palace Road
Hammersmith, London W6 8JB

The website address is:
www.thorsonselement.com

and *HarperElement* are trademarks of
HarperCollins*Publishers* Limited

Published by HarperElement 2005
This edition published 2005

4

© Jane Elliott 2005

Jane Elliott asserts the moral right to
be identified as the author of this work

A catalogue record for this book
is available from the British Library

ISBN 0 00 720893 6

Printed and bound in Great Britain by
Clays Ltd, St Ives plc

All rights reserved. No part of this publication may be
reproduced, stored in a retrieval system, or transmitted,
in any form or by any means, electronic, mechanical,
photocopying, recording or otherwise, without the prior
written permission of the publishers.

Evil is unspectacular and always human,
and shares our bed and eats at our table.

W. H. Auden

A Note from the Author

As a child I never thought anyone would believe what I had to say, so when my book went straight to number one in the hardback bestseller charts and everyone was talking about how brave I was to tell my story, I found it hard to take in. One minute I would be hugging myself with excitement, and the next I would be frightened of what might happen now I'd let the genie out of the bottle.

Initially I wanted to write the book because I knew how much I'd been helped by reading *A Child Called It* by Dave Pelzer. If just one child who was being abused read my story, I reasoned, and felt inspired enough to speak out and end the cycle of bullying in their own life, it would be worth doing.

Every time my publishers rang to say they were printing more copies to meet the demand, I imagined how many more people would be reading it and maybe seeing that it was possible for them to turn on the bullies and regain control of their lives.

The actual writing process was hard because it stirred up one or two memories and emotions that I'd been trying to forget about. But now I've shouted out to the whole world all the things I was told had to be kept secret, it feels as though a lead weight has been lifted off my shoulders.

However hard I'd been trying to suppress the memories over the years, they were always there. I could distract myself with family chores, a bottle of wine or a packet of cigarettes, but that didn't make the hurt go away for more than a few hours. Facing up to the memories and telling the whole story was like opening the curtains and windows on a sunny day and letting light and a fresh breeze into a dark room, stale with poisonous air.

One of my biggest worries was how my children would react to the book. They're both still young and although they knew that something bad had happened in my childhood they didn't know any details. I've told them the book contains material they might find upsetting and that I would rather they didn't read it until they were older, and so far they've managed to resist the temptation – I think. The excitement of hearing their mum talking on the radio and seeing the book all over the shelves in the supermarket and W H Smith seems to have more than compensated them for any worries it might have caused them.

The hard thing for them is that they're not allowed to tell their friends about it. This was particularly tough when it was at the top of the charts and they were longing to share the excitement that was going on within our little family group. But they're all too aware of the dangers of disclosing my true identity and of my whereabouts being discovered by my family. They saw what happened to their mum last time her brothers caught up with her, and they don't want to take the risk of that happening again. They keep telling me how proud of me they are. I just hope they realize how proud I am of them as well.

My husband has also had to adjust from being the sole worker in the family to having to stay home a lot to look after the girls while I was off at publishers' meetings and giving interviews, but there have been some big compensations for him too. The sense of satisfaction I got from seeing how well the book was doing made me a lot easier to live with (not that I'm not still a bit of a nightmare for him some days!), and we have been able to pay off a few of the debts we were building up and improve our lives materially.

I don't think he really believed the book would be a great success any more than I did, but it's surprising how quickly we both got used to having a number one hit and started to feel disappointed when it got knocked down to number two or three!

The charts are full of stories of childhood abuse now and there have been a lot of articles in the press speculating on why so many people want to read about such a difficult subject. I don't think it is the abuse they want to hear about, but the fact that some of the children who suffer from it manage to survive and ultimately triumph. They want to be shocked at the start of the book, crying in the middle and exultant at the end.

I suspect that the audiences for books like *The Little Prisoner* fall into two categories. Firstly there are those who come from stable, happy homes, who can't understand how anyone can abuse a child, and want to find out about a world they can barely imagine. Secondly, there are those who suffered something similar themselves and find some comfort in discovering they are not alone in the world. They get some inspiration from discovering that not only is it possible to go on to lead happy and normal lives, but that you can actually turn all that misery into something positive.

I have a horrible feeling there are more people in the second category than anyone really wants to admit, and as long as the subject remains shrouded in secrecy and is considered a taboo to talk about, we'll never know the full extent of the problem. With the popularity of books like mine, however, at least we have started to open the curtains and let a little light into these darkest and nastiest of corners.

If we don't all understand what is going on in families like the one I came from, we can't hope to make things better.

Prologue

When people talk about evil they are usually thinking of mass murderers like the fictional Hannibal Lecter or dictators like Adolf Hitler, but for most of us our actual encounters with evil are more mundane. There are the school playground bullies and sadistic teachers who turn their victims' days into nightmares, the unkind care workers in the old people's homes or the violent thieves who invade the lives of the elderly or infirm. Our brushes with these evils are usually passing or second-hand, but none the less chilling for that.

This, however, is the true story of a four-year-old girl who fell into the power of a man for whom evil was a relentless daily activity. She remained in his power for seventeen years until she eventually managed to escape and turn the tables. It is a story of terror and abuse on a scale that is almost unbelievable, but it also tells of her enormous act of courage which led to the arrest, trial and imprisonment of her persecutor.

Most of us don't usually hear about children like Jane until we read about their deaths in the papers and then we all wonder how such things could be going on under our noses and under the noses of all the welfare workers who are supposed to be there to help. We try to imagine what can have gone wrong, but we can't because these children live in a world that is unimaginable to anyone who hasn't been there. This is the story of a survivor and we should all listen to what she has to tell us.

Jane Elliott's story is almost unbearable to read in parts, but it needs to be told because the people who perpetrate these sorts of crimes rely on the silence of their victims. If people talk openly about what happens behind closed doors, then evil on the scale of what happened to Jane becomes harder to achieve. Bullies can only operate when other people are too frightened, ashamed or embarrassed to talk about what is being done to them. By telling her story, Jane is making it a little harder for evil to prosper in future.

The names of the characters have all been changed to protect Jane's identity and the identities of those who helped her in her fight for justice.

Introduction

I was being led back into the courtroom by a victim liaison officer, an elderly lady. Up till then they had been careful to take me in and out of a different door from Richard, my stepfather, or if they hadn't then they had made sure we didn't meet, which was making me feel more confident. Hiding behind my hair, I had still been able to avoid seeing him and remembering his face too clearly. As I came back in through the door with my head down I saw a pair of shoes directly ahead of me, blocking my way. I looked up, straight into a face that made me feel sick with fear. The pale snakelike eyes and the ginger hair were the same, although he looked a little stockier than I remembered him.

'Get me out of here,' I hissed through gritted teeth, feeling his eyes boring into mine and his thoughts getting back inside my head. 'Get me out, get me out.'

'Calm down, for heaven's sake,' the lady said, irritated by such a show of emotion. 'Come through here.'

She led me into a room off the court, which had a glass door. He followed us, but didn't come in, standing outside the glass, just staring at me with no expression.

'Get the police!' I screamed. 'Get the police!'

'Don't be silly, dear.' She was losing patience now. 'Who is it you're worried about? Is it him?' She gestured towards the immobile figure on the other side of the glass with the dead, staring eyes.

'Get someone!' I screamed and she realized there was no way she could calm me down. She walked towards the door. 'Don't leave me!' I screamed, suddenly envisaging him and me in the room alone. The woman was panicking now, aware that she didn't know how to handle the situation.

At that moment Marie and another police officer arrived. Finding me standing in the corner of the room, hiding my face against the wall like a child in trouble, they came to the rescue, furious with everyone and getting me to safety.

'He's going to kill me,' I moaned as Marie put her arm round me. 'I'm dead.'

'No, he won't, Jane,' she soothed me. 'He can't do anything now. You're doing fine. It's nearly over.'

Chapter One

Early childhood memories don't always remain in the right order or come back the moment they're called, preferring to remain stubbornly locked in secret compartments deep in the filing cabinets of my mind. Sometimes I can picture a scene clearly from as young as three or four, but I can't remember why I was there or what happened next. Every now and then the lost memories will return unexpectedly and often it would have been better if they'd remained lost. I have a horrible feeling that there are still some compartments for which my subconscious has deliberately lost the key, fearing that I won't be able to cope with what would come out, but which one day will allow themselves to be forced open like others before them. It is as if they wait until they know I will be strong enough to cope with whatever is revealed. I don't look forward to seeing what's inside them.

I can't always piece together the order that things happened in either. I might be able to remember that I was a certain size at the time that some event occurred, but be unable to tell if I was four or six. I might be able to remember something that was a regular occurrence, but be unable to say whether it went on for a year or three years, whether it was every week or every month. I suppose it doesn't matter very much, but this confusion makes it difficult to give a truly factual account of the early years of my life, since anyone else who might be able to remember those times will probably have reasons not to tell the truth, or at least to adjust it to make their role in it more bearable.

I do remember being in care with my little brother Jimmy. I must have been about three when we were taken away from home and he would have been about eighteen months younger, so still little more than a baby. I loved Jimmy more than anything in the world. My dad tells me that when he used to come and take us out of the children's home for a pub lunch or some such outing, I would act like a little mother to Jimmy, feeding him and fussing over him. I don't recall the outings, but I do recall how much I adored Jimmy.

The main things I remember about the children's home were the brown vitamin tablets they used to dispense to us each morning in little purple cups, and being made to eat Brussels sprouts and hating every damp mouthful as they gradually grew colder and more inedible on my plate.

There was one woman working there who used to single me out from the evening line-up, after we had all been given our glasses of milk, and take me somewhere private, putting her finger to her lips as if we had a secret from the rest of the world. Then she would sit me down and comb my long hair, spending ages curling it and making me feel beautiful and special for a few minutes each day. (My hair was so dark and fine that people were always asking me if I was Indian or Pakistani.) When she'd finished her work the woman would give me a hand mirror to hold up in front of me so I could see the back of my head in the mirror on the wall and admire her handiwork. It seemed like a magic mirror to me.

Most of the information I picked up later about those early years and why we were taken away from home came to me because Mum was always happy to talk about me to other people as if I wasn't there. I'd be sitting quietly in the corner of the room, waiting for an instruction as to my next duty, while she would be holding forth to some neighbour or other. Every so often she would remember I was there and remind me, 'Don't you ever let him know I told you that.' My stepfather didn't like anyone to talk about the past.

When I was in my mid-twenties I tracked Dad down and he's told me a few things, but I don't like to keep asking him questions. It seems that Dad had a bit of a drinking problem, which Mum made worse by playing around with other blokes and generally giving him a hard time. He had already left us before we were taken into care and Mum had started going out with Richard, or 'Silly Git', as I prefer to think of him. He might even have been living with us by then, although he would have been very young, no more than sixteen or seventeen. He's only fourteen years older than me.

Jimmy and I were sent to a couple of different foster homes, one of which I think must have been quite nice, since I can't remember much about it. The second one wasn't so good. They seemed like evil people to me, but perhaps they were just very strict in a way I wasn't used to. We were never allowed to whisper to each other, or speak unless we were spoken to, and when they caught me whispering to Jimmy one time they stuck a piece of tape over my mouth which had been holding together a pair of newly bought socks. I had to sit at the top of the stairs with the tape over my mouth all night while everyone else in the house went to bed.

Even though I wasn't having a good time in the foster family, I still never wanted to go back home, but I wouldn't have been able to explain to anyone why not.

'I'm really looking forward to coming home,' I would tell Mum when I saw her, but I absolutely wasn't.

When we went back home for visits there was an atmosphere in the house that made me frightened, although nothing bad actually happened in those few hours. I would sit very quietly, not wanting to make the new man of the house angry, but Jimmy had no such inhibitions and from the moment we were dropped off he would scream with what sounded like terror. I could tell it made Richard angry and that frightened me even more, but nothing I could do would calm Jimmy down until the social workers came to take us back. We would just sit together on the sofa for the whole visit with him screaming and me trying to comfort him. Richard's anger and our mother's desperation would swell to what felt like dangerous proportions as they waited for the ordeal of the visit to be over.

Jimmy had a large scar right around his forehead, which has stayed with him into adulthood. I was always told that he got it from falling against the coffee table before we were taken into care. I accepted the story at the time, but thinking back now, it's an awfully big scar to get from bumping into a table. He was only tiny, so it wasn't as if he had far to fall, or much weight behind him. I wonder now if something more serious happened to him and that was why we were taken into care and why he was always so terrified to go back home. I don't suppose I'll ever know now because Jimmy was too little to remember.

Someone told me that we were taken into care because we were being generally neglected, that we had vivid, sore 'potty rings' from where we had been left too long on our pots, but everyone seems to be vague about the details.

Before we went into care we'd lived in a flat, but by the time my memories start to kick in Mum and Richard had moved to a council house. Maybe that was how they managed to convince the authorities that they were fit to have me back. They'd also had a baby boy of their own, called Pete, which must have made them look like a more normal family, like people who had mended their ways, matured and accepted their responsibilities. Richard was, after all, still a teenager, but there might have been a case for believing that he had now grown up enough to be put in charge of children.

I sometimes wonder whether Mum and Richard would have taken me back if I'd made as much fuss as Jimmy. Now I wish I'd given it a go, since Jimmy ended up being adopted by kind people, but at the time it seemed too dangerous to make Richard angry and I preferred to remain docile and well-behaved in his presence.

Years later I discovered that they had told the authorities they 'only wanted the girl'. I couldn't believe it, but Jimmy's files later confirmed it. Jimmy had read the files himself and felt deeply rejected, even when I assured him that he'd had the luckiest escape of his life.

I also heard Mum boasting that our family had slipped a bribe to someone in the local authority to allow me home and that two senior people had resigned when they heard that I was being returned to 'that hell-hole', as it was described in some report. My missing files would make interesting reading, but it isn't really important what happened in those first few years, because the real horrors were only just about to begin.

One of the scenes that has always remained clear in my head was saying goodbye to Jimmy on the doorstep of the foster home. He was crying and I wanted to as well, but didn't dare to show my feelings to anyone. Someone had told me that Jimmy would be coming back home as well in a couple of weeks, but I didn't believe it. I think I must have overheard something that told me they were lying. I knew they were going to separate us and it broke my heart. I'd hated it at the foster home, but at least I'd had Jimmy with me. Now I was going to be moved to somewhere else where I felt bad things would be happening and I wouldn't even have him to cuddle and talk to.

I still didn't tell Mum any of these thoughts; I just told her that I couldn't wait to get home. I didn't want to hurt her feelings. Little children only want to please their parents if they can.

From the moment Jimmy and I were parted I used to try to communicate with him telepathically whenever I was on my own. I had a birthmark on my arm which I convinced myself looked like the letter 'J', so I would stare at it and try to talk to Jimmy in my mind, telling him to be a good boy and assuring him that I would come to see him soon, asking him what sort of day he had had and telling him all about mine. I never did see him again until we had both grown up and grown apart, but at the time it comforted me a little to think I was still connected to him.

After Pete, Mum and Richard had three more boys, one almost every year, but none of them could take Jimmy's place in my heart. I had to keep this quiet because I was never allowed to talk about him again. It was as if he had never existed in our lives. We had a lot of secrets like that. I was never allowed to tell anyone that Richard was my stepfather, not my real father, although anyone living in the neighbourhood must have known. My four half-brothers never realized that I wasn't their full sister until I was in my late twenties and the court case brought everything to light. I was never allowed to have any contact with any of my relations on my father's side; it was as if they didn't exist. I have no memory of my grandparents on that side at all. It was as if Richard wanted to keep control of exactly what information was allowed.

My dad tells me that he tried to come and visit me in the house a few times, but was met with such violence and abuse that he decided it would be safer for me if he stayed away and allowed things to calm down. That seemed like the last of my potential allies gone, although I later discovered he had tried to keep an eye on what was happening to me in other ways.

One day a photograph of Jimmy fell out from behind another picture in an album.

'Who's that? Who's that? Who's that?' one of my little brothers asked.

Richard immediately became angry, throwing the picture in the bin and making it clear that there were to be no more questions about the little boy in the photograph. Jimmy was no longer part of our family.

Any house we lived in inevitably became a gleaming domestic fortress. I guess that another reason why Mum and Richard were able to convince the authorities that they would be good parents to me now was that they kept their home spotlessly clean and totally secure. My stepfather was obsessed with decorating; there was never a day when he wasn't redoing one room or another with new flock wallpaper, the sort you see inside old-fashioned pubs, or applying another coat of paint, or putting up pine cladding or building fake brick fireplaces. I even used to cover my schoolbooks in the offcuts from old rolls of his flock wallpaper.

Our privacy was everything to him. Net curtains covered the windows during the day and would be reinforced by expensive thick lined velvet curtains as soon as the light outside started to fade. God knows where they got the money to buy them, but they ordered them from catalogues. There could never be a chink left in our armour, anything that would allow prying eyes the slightest opportunity to see inside our private lives. Outside the houses would be gates, high fences and even higher conifers. Locks and bolts would ensure that no one, not even members of the family, could get in and out easily. Richard's control over his domain was total. Our houses were always the 'nicest' in the area.

All of us did housework all the time. Not a speck of dust or dirt ever escaped Richard's eagle eye. If a bit of fluff came off one of our socks onto the carpet we were immediately screamed at to pick it up, so we would pad around in slippers to be on the safe side. Visitors could never believe that anyone could keep a house with children in so clean and tidy. Every kitchen cupboard would have to be emptied and wiped down every day, every item of furniture moved and cleaned and replaced, even the cooker and the fridge. Ledges above doors and windows that would normally be out of sight and out of mind were wiped down every single day. We sparkled and shone like an army barracks ruled over by a sergeant major prone to terrifying rages. The stairs had to be brushed by hand each morning and Mum would then vacuum them three or four times more during the course of the day.

The garden received just as much attention, the edges of the lawn having to be trimmed with scissors.

But doing housework was a way of keeping busy and out of Richard's way in case he was in one of his moods.

Richard was about four years younger than Mum and only eighteen when I was taken back home, but to me he was still a fully grown adult and I knew that to answer him back or disobey him in any way would be to endanger all our safety. Children know these things instinctively, just as they know which teachers they can play up at school and which ones will never tolerate any bad behaviour. Even though I'd hated being made to take tablets at the children's home, I'd never been frightened to fight back against the staff administering them, but something about this man told me that if I fought back or protested in any way, things would become a thousand times worse.

He didn't look like a monster, although he was over six feet tall, slim and muscular. He had ginger hair and pale snakelike eyes and always dressed casually but smartly. He took great care of his appearance, just like his home. I ironed his clothes so often over the years I can remember exactly what he owned: the neatly pressed pairs of jeans and polo shirts, the v-necked jumpers and Farrahs trousers. When I got older my friends sometimes used to tell me they fancied him, which made me want to be sick because to me he seemed the ugliest thing in the world. He had a tattoo of Mum's name on his neck to show the world how tough he was.

The moment I was swallowed up into the house and invisible to the outside world, he made his hatred of me plain. Every time he passed me when Mum wasn't looking he'd slap me, pinch me, kick me or pull my hair so hard I thought it would come out at the roots. He would lean his lips close to my ears and hiss how much he loathed me while his fingers squeezed my face painfully like a vice.

'I hate you, you little Paki bastard,' he would spit. 'Everything was good here until you came back, you little cunt! You are so fucking ugly. You wait till later.'

His hatred for me seemed to be so powerful he could hardly control himself. To call me a 'Paki' was the worst insult he could think of, since he carried his racist views proudly, like badges of honour.

He took to spitting in my food whenever he had the opportunity and I would have to mix the spittle into the mash or the gravy to make it possible to swallow, since he would force me to eat every last scrap.

'You ain't leaving the table until you've eaten every mouthful,' he'd say, as if he was merely a concerned parent worrying about his child's diet, but all the time he would be grinning because he knew what he had done.

When my brother Pete was old enough to talk he saw it happen one time.

'Er, Dad,' he screeched, 'why did you spit in Janey's food?'

'Don't be stupid,' he snapped. 'I didn't.'

When I saw that Mum's attention had been caught, thinking I had a witness in little Pete, I found enough courage to say, 'Yes, he did. He always does.' But she couldn't believe anyone would do such a disgusting thing and so from then on Richard was able to turn it into a double-bluff, making loud hawking noises over my plate and then dropping even larger globs of phlegm into it when my mother looked away, tutting irritably and telling him 'not to be so stupid', as if it was no more than a joke that she no longer found funny.

I think she must have known how much he hated me, though, because she never seemed to like to leave me alone in a room with him for any length of time when I was tiny. If she could see he was in a mood and she had to go to the toilet, she would call me to come with her, a bit like calling a dog to heel. When we got inside she would make me sit down in front of her with my back to her knees while she did her business. I can't think of any other reason why she would have done that, but we never spoke about it and I was always happy to go with her, knowing that it was saving me from a slap or a kick. What she never realized, however, was that

Richard didn't have to be in a mood to hit me or punch me or hiss insults into my ear – he did it all the time.

The house had three bedrooms, so I had a room of my own from the start and it was beautifully decorated, just as a little girl's bedroom should be. To begin with my wallpaper was 'Sarah Jane' with pictures of a little girl in a big floppy hat, then it was changed for a Pierrot design, and later a pattern of horses. I had loads of toys, too, but I was never allowed to play with them unless I did Richard some 'favour' in return.

These favours became my way of life. If Mum let me go out to play while Richard was out somewhere and he came home and found me outside, then I would 'owe him a favour'. If I wanted to eat a sweet or go to a friend's birthday party or watch *The Muppet Show*, he might say yes, but would let me know that I would be paying him back with a favour later. In the end I stopped asking for anything, but he would still demand the favours or call them 'punishments' for some 'crime' instead, like being rude or sulky. Looking back now I realize that he was going to make me do the favours anyway, so I wish I had got more in exchange for them, but I wasn't able to see so clearly what was happening at the time. He managed to make it all so confusing and frightening.

My favourite toy was Wolfie, a giant teddy with a dog's head, which was almost as big as me. Wolfie had braces which I used to slip my arms through so he would dance with me and walk around the room. He was my best friend.

If Mum was in the house when Richard wanted to punish me he would whisper in my ear, 'Watch this.' He would then start shouting at me about something and shouting at my mum about what a moody cow I was. Seeing the sort of temper he was in, Mum would agree with him, tutting sadly at what a tiresome girl I was. Richard would then kick me and slap me and drag me upstairs by my ponytail, making me lose my footing so that I was literally being dragged by my hair. He would tell Mum that he was going to put me to bed and give me 'a good talking to' and would then beat me even more viciously once we got there.

'Wait till your Mum goes out,' he'd tell me as he crushed my face between his fingers, 'then you'll get it.'

In the beginning when he used to hit me with his hand, a slipper or a stick, I would always cry. Quite soon, however, I decided that I wouldn't give him the satisfaction any more. I couldn't stop my eyes from watering up with the pain, but I found that if I just clenched my teeth and stared at him I could stop myself from actually crying. It was the only little bit of defiance I could find the courage or strength for, and it often made the beatings worse.

'Not crying?' he would say. 'Isn't it fucking hurting enough then?'

But then when I had cried he would become even angrier and tell me he was going to 'give me something to cry about'. I guess he was always going to do whatever he wanted, regardless of what I did or said.

I think Mum knew that he was going too far sometimes, because after he had put me to bed she would sometimes creep into my room to check that I was still breathing. I used to breathe really shallowly, just to give her a fright and to punish her for letting him hurt me. It was a mean thing to do, but I was cross with her.

'Janey, Janey,' she would whisper and I would open my eyes suddenly, as if I had been asleep. 'Breathe properly,' she would scold me, angry that I had frightened her. She never raised her voice because she didn't want Richard to know that she had come up to check I was alive. Although I was angry with her for not helping me, I was also relieved that she wasn't getting beaten up herself.

Other times Richard would tell me what he and I were going to do later and if I didn't look pleased, or turned away or cried, he would say, 'Right, you ungrateful bitch, now look what I'm gonna do. I'll teach you.' He would then start rowing with Mum and beat her up in front of me.

'The only reason your mum and me ever argue is because of you,' he would tell me over and over again, and I believed him, the guilt weighing heavily on my soul. I learnt that I must always agree with him, always smile and always be grateful for everything or there would be terrible punishments for me and my mum.

Like a small boy pulling the wings off insects, or stuffing them into jam jars and watching them starve or suffocate, Richard seemed to enjoy making me suffer for no reason at all. The airing cupboard for the house was in my room and he used to like to make me strip my clothes off and crawl inside amongst the piles of towels. I don't know how long he left me in there, because time is immeasurable when you are small and frightened and sitting in the dark, and I don't know if the door had a lock on it, because I never had the nerve to try to get out until he told me I could. Disobeying orders would have brought a far worse punishment down on my head. The rule was to endure whatever he told me to endure, and to do so with a cheerful smile and gratitude. Being a 'sulky cow' was one of the worst 'crimes' I could commit. He would sometimes come back just to check I hadn't fainted from the heat, then he would shut the door again and leave me in the dark once more with no idea how much longer I would be there.

There was a ledge in my room too and I remember being made to stand on it, but I can't remember what happened next. One day that memory will probably return as well, but I'm not looking forward to it.

These physical humiliations and discomforts, however, were not as unsettling as the mind games, which started almost immediately I came back home.

'Go and turn the hot water on for me, Janey,' Mum would say and I would run upstairs to the immersion.

'Go and turn the hot water off,' Richard would tell me as soon as I got back from turning it on. I would know to obey without saying anything.

'Why didn't you turn the water on when I asked you?' Mum would want to know a little while later when she went up for her bath.

'I did,' I would protest. 'He told me to turn it off again.'

'You bloody little liar!' he would explode and I would have no chance of convincing Mum that I was telling the truth once he started ranting and raving. If I'd argued any further I would have got a beating, so I just stayed quiet, knowing it wouldn't be long before he thought of another game.

When it came to the beatings Richard liked to vary the implements he used. Sometimes it was a slipper, or a hand or a bamboo stick. He would make me choose which it was to be. As I got older the beatings got less, perhaps because they had served their purpose in training me to obey him. Instead I would just be punched or smacked around the head or thrown across the room or made to pay a forfeit by doing a favour. Whatever happened, I would never be let off a punishment.

'Do you want breakfast, Jane?' Mum called through from the kitchen one morning to where I was sitting on the sofa in the front room.

'Yes please,' I called back.

'No, you don't,' my stepfather hissed from the nearby armchair. 'Tell her you don't want any.'

'No, I don't want any really,' I shouted.

'Why not?' Mum asked, appearing in the doorway.

'She must be fucking mad,' he yelled, jumping up from his chair. 'She doesn't know what she fucking wants. Do you want fucking breakfast or not?'

'Yes, please,' I said in a small confused voice.

'What do you want?' Mum asked, shaking her head in puzzlement.

'Toast,' I said and she went back to the kitchen to make it for me.

The moment she was out of sight Richard's fingers closed painfully round my face like a clamp and he was whispering again, his face inches from mine. 'I told you, you don't want any fucking breakfast. Now fucking tell her.'

'I don't want any toast, Mum,' I obediently called out to the kitchen. 'I don't really want anything.'

'Stop messing me about, Jane!' she shouted.

'Stop messing your mum about!' Richard screamed, hitting me hard around the head. 'She's fucking mad,' he called out to Mum. 'She just likes stirring up fucking arguments!'

He was always playing these mind games to make Mum angry with me and to give him an excuse to smack me around. I just ended up so confused.

I know which memory is the first one I can find which has a sexual connection, but I think there may be even earlier ones lying in wait beneath the dust somewhere. This one must have happened a couple of years after I came back home because I remember I was sharing a bed with my brother Pete. My next brother, Dan, was also in with us in a separate bed. I'd been turned out of my room because it was having one of its routine redecorations and Pete and I were lying top to tail in his bed. The reason I think something must have happened before is because I remember I was awake and listening that night, terrified of what was about to happen. I'd heard my mother going out, the front door shutting after her, and I'd known that Richard would soon be upstairs to get me.

Every sound told me a story. The living-room door opened downstairs and I could sense Richard's stealthy footsteps on the stairs. I closed my eyes, trying to stop my body from shaking so that I could pretend to be asleep. I thought maybe I would be safe because Pete was lying beside me and Richard wouldn't want to wake him up. I was always clutching at straws like that to give myself some hope, and I was always disappointed.

I could tell the door was opening beside my head and I could feel Richard moving me about to wake me up. I opened my eyes and looked at him.

'Come out here,' he whispered, 'quietly.'

I climbed out of the warm bed, leaving Pete sleeping peacefully, and Richard closed the door behind me. I stood on the landing, waiting as he shut the other doors on the landing and knelt down in front of me.

'We're going to play a little game,' he said. 'Shut your eyes and don't you dare open them.'

I obeyed him without question and heard him unzipping his trousers.

'Don't open your eyes,' he repeated. 'We're going to play the game now.'

I nodded, not wanting to make him angry.

'I want you to play with my thumb. You hold it, and stroke it and move it up and down, and something magic will happen.'

I knew it wasn't his thumb that he put into my hand, which also makes me think something must have happened before that, but I played along and pretended, just as he had told me. The more co-operative I was, I thought, the sooner I could get back to bed and the more likely I was to avoid a beating.

'What is it you're holding?' he asked every so often as I worked away.

'Your thumb,' I replied obediently and then the magic happened and he told me to go to the bathroom to wash my hands. Some of his mess had spilled on the carpet and he rubbed at it with his foot, making the scratching noise that I would hear so many times over the coming years.

As I came back out of the bathroom I looked at the patch of disturbed pile on the carpet and couldn't believe that Mum wouldn't notice it when she got home. As the years went by more and more of these patches would appear, reminding me every time I walked past of the things I'd had to do.

'Do you want something to eat then?' Richard asked, and I nodded. 'Come downstairs and I'll make you some toast and tea.'

He was really nice to me that time, just as if we had been playing a game that we'd both enjoyed, but he wasn't always so pleasant after he'd had his way. One night he took me into the kitchen and grabbed the long wooden-handled carving knife from the drawer, pinned me against the wall and pressed the razor-sharp blade against my neck.

'If you ever tell anybody what we've done I'll kill you,' he snarled in my face, 'and then I'll kill your mum and no one will ever know because I'll just tell them you both ran away.'

I believed he was capable of it because I'd seen how hard he beat Mum when she made him angry, slamming her head against the floor or the walls and smashing chairs down on her while I sat on the sofa watching and hugging my little brothers as they screamed. He would always tell me that it was my fault, and I believed him. I felt so guilty, and I was terrified he would kill Mum and then I would have no one to protect me from him at all.

Almost as soon as I got back home I was old enough to go to infant school. I loved everything about it, but most of all I loved the fact that it allowed me to get out of the house and be with people who appeared to like me. All through my school years there were several people who seemed to go out of their way to talk to me and ask me how I was. Only later did I discover that they were friends of my dad's and that they were trying to find out if I was alright for him. Right from the beginning one of my friends' mothers was reporting back to him. Because I was always so happy at school, and because I didn't carry any visible signs of abuse, they were able to report back that all was well. If only I had known that, I could have communicated with my dad through them and maybe he would have found a way to get me out of that house.

I think there must have been some people who had an idea about some of the things going on in the house, though, because social workers would come to the door sometimes, but Richard would physically throw them out and I never knew what happened after that because when the police went to look for my files years later they'd disappeared. None of the social workers ever came to speak to me. I can't blame them if they were frightened off; Richard frightened almost everyone. I dare say there were people around who were as physically strong or even stronger than him, but when he went into one of his blind rages he lost all his inhibitions and very few people were able to match his levels of aggression and viciousness.

Family life provides so many little opportunities for grown ups to inflict pain on their children if they so choose. Mum always bathed us when we were little, but a couple of times Richard got to do it. I guess Mum was ill or too heavily pregnant and he was able to make it sound as if he was doing her a favour by taking over this chore.

One night he told me he was going to wash my hair and I was trembling with fear as we went upstairs, wondering what horrors he had planned. There was no way out. Stepping into the bath I was like a condemned man walking up the steps to the guillotine. Everything went as it should for a few minutes and I stayed as quiet and happy-looking as I could manage. Richard was giving no clues as to when he might pounce or how, but I wasn't fooled, I knew it was coming.

When it was time to wet my hair I felt his hand gripping me tightly. He pushed my head under the water and held it there, no doubt enjoying the feeling of having the power of life or death over me. As I fought for breath and the water rushed into my mouth, I thought I was going to die, that he had finally decided he hated me so much he was going to kill me. My childish struggles were useless against the strength of his hands and only served to make him angrier.

After what seemed like an age he pulled me up into the air by my hair, squeezing my face painfully as I wailed and hitting me round the head.

'Shut up and stop screaming!' he hissed through gritted teeth.

I forced myself to be silent as he washed my hair as though nothing was wrong, knowing that in a few minutes I was going to have to rinse the soap out and certain he wouldn't be able to resist the temptation of repeating the attack. When the moment came I tried to hold onto both sides of the bath, but he ordered me to loosen my fingers and pushed me back under the water again, infuriated even further by this futile attempt at self-defence, this challenge to his power. I came up a few seconds later, spluttering and screaming, and he put his hand over my nose and mouth, swearing in my ear to shut me up. He then dragged me painfully out of the bath, gripping my arms so hard I thought he would crush them and banging my legs on the hard edges.

'Get your pyjamas on!' he shouted and I obeyed, relieved to be out of the water and still alive.

I went downstairs to the front room on wobbly legs and when I saw Mum I burst into tears.

'What's wrong with you?' she asked.

'He tried to drown me,' I replied.

He must have heard me and came charging into the room, screaming and shouting about how naughty I had been, how I had refused to have my hair washed and had made a fuss when the soap went into my eyes.

'Oh, she never likes having her hair washed,' Mum agreed. It was always easier for her to agree with him if she didn't want to get a beating herself.

I was sent to bed with a smack for being so unco-operative.

Sometimes when I was in the bath Richard would put a ladder up the side of the house and look in the window, treating it as a joke. Mum would laugh, too, telling me I had to get over feeling shy about myself. Richard always managed to make it sound as though he was doing everything for my own good, as though everything that happened to me was my own fault.

When we were little we were only allowed to have baths on Sunday evenings and always had to share the water in order to keep the bills down. As I got bigger Richard started to let me have one during the week as well. Sometimes he would come down from having his own bath and tell me to have one in his water. He would always leave something that looked like semen floating on top of the water. The first time it happened I tried to get out of it by wetting my hair in the basin to look as if I'd had a bath, but he came upstairs to check on me. He opened the door and smirked at me as I climbed into his filthy water, no doubt knowing how disgusted I was. When I came downstairs afterwards I was quiet and 'sulky' so I got a good hiding and was sent back up to bed.

When I was seven I decided that I couldn't face going home any more. The time had come to run away. I used to daydream about escaping all the time, but when it actually came to doing it things seemed to become more complicated. I was convinced at that stage that Richard could read my mind and that he would be able to tell what I was planning, which made me doubly anxious.

Sometimes he did seem to know things that I was sure I'd never told him. Only years later did I realize that they were things I'd told my mum and that she must have passed them on to him, betraying my confidence every time.

Other times he would trick confessions out of me. 'I know you was mucking about at school today,' he would tell me when I got home, 'because the school board woman came round.'

I would rack my brain for the slightest thing I might have done which could have resulted in being reported like this. Filled with guilt as I always was, it wasn't hard to find something and to convince myself that Richard truly did know everything. Believing it was hopeless to try to resist his powers, I would admit that I had been bad and he would then be free to punish me in whatever way he pleased. I doubt if I ever really did do anything very bad at school, apart perhaps from talking too much.

I had a friend at school called Lucy and had told her about my stepdad beating me and threatening to kill me. I hadn't told her about any of the other stuff; that would have been too embarrassing. Lucy said she wanted to run away as well, although I don't think she was having any particular problems at home, just fancied an adventure. I wasn't trying to escape from school, because I really liked my teacher, but it seemed more sensible to us to go during the lunch hour, when we were less likely to be missed, than to wait until the end of the day.

'I want to take my sister with us as well,' Lucy told me as we were laying our escape plans. Her sister was in the infant school, which was next door to the junior school where we were in our first year.

'How are we going to get her?' I asked.

'I'll tell her dinner lady that she has a dentist's appointment,' Lucy explained, apparently confident that this would work.

I waited in the bushes beside the playground while she disappeared into the infant school. I was so excited by the prospect of finally getting away that my heart was thumping.

A few minutes after going in Lucy reappeared and came running across the playground towards me.

'The dinner lady didn't believe me,' she panted. 'She went to check, so I had to run for it.'

'We'll have to go without your sister,' I said, and she nodded her agreement.

We ran as fast as we could to get out of the area of the school, which wasn't easy for me because I had such stupid shoes. Silly Git always went with me to buy my clothes and shoes and for some reason he wouldn't let me go into the shop that sold sensible school shoes. He always made me buy high-heeled court shoes with pointed toes and then insisted on putting blakeys (those little metal tips) on the heels so that I would make a noise when I walked in them and everyone would turn round to look as I went clacking past on my skinny little legs. I suppose it must have turned him on or something, but I kept twisting my ankles because I wasn't used to walking in heels. He didn't care about details like that. Lucy was always really keen to borrow my shoes, believing them to be the height of sophistication. I would have been happy never to have seen them again as long as I lived.

By the time school was over we had managed to get a long way away and had reached a row of shops on a new estate.

'I'm really hungry,' I complained. 'Have you got any money?'

'I've only got five pence that my mum gave me for crisps,' Lucy said dubiously. 'That won't get us far. We'll have to nick something.'

I'd never stolen anything in my life and the thought of it filled me with horror. What if we were caught? They would be bound to take us home and that would give Richard the perfect excuse to beat me half to death. But hunger got the better of my fears and we went into a little supermarket to see what we could get. We must have been looking very suspicious, hanging around for too long, because the woman behind the till threw us out, by which time Lucy had managed to steal a cake but I had only managed to get a plastic Jif lemon, having panicked and grabbed the first thing that came to hand.

'Can I try your shoes?' Lucy asked as we sat munching on the cake in a nearby underpass.

I agreed happily, since my feet were hurting from walking so far in them. We changed socks at the same time, so that I could have her long ones with pictures of the Flintstones up the sides, and then continued on our way.

I was desperate for the toilet, but there was nowhere else to go other than beside the path. I was just getting down to business when a woman came round the corner with her kids. Unable to run away, I had to answer her questions about where our parents were and whether they knew we were there. I don't suppose my answers were very convincing. She eventually went away, but I suspect she was planning to ring the police the moment she got to a phone.

We continued on our journey and by the time we reached open fields it was starting to get dark. Lucy was beginning to talk about the possibility of going home, but then she didn't have anything to be afraid of when she got there. I knew that my parents would have been told of my disappearance by now and that I was going to be in serious trouble. I wanted to keep walking forever. I didn't care how dark or cold it got, nothing could be as frightening as stepping through my own front door.

Some bigger children were coming out of a senior school and we had to walk past a bunch of them. They were all staring. I guess we must have looked like the runaways we were. There wasn't much chance that we were going to get away with our break for freedom for much longer and in fact the next figures who appeared out of the darkness were a couple of police officers. A terrible fear gripped me when I realized they were going to take me home. I would rather have lived in the woods forever than take another beating. But I could tell Lucy was quite relieved to have been found before night set in.

The police told us off for all the trouble and worry we had caused everyone and escorted us back to their car.

'Why did you run away?' one of them asked as we drove towards home.

'Her dad says he's going to kill her,' Lucy replied, 'and he beats her all the time.'

Just when I thought things couldn't get any worse, they had.

'Is that true?' the policeman asked.

'No,' I shook my head. 'I was lying when I told her that. It never happened.'

I looked down at the floor to avoid his eyes and realized we were still wearing the wrong shoes and socks. I would be in even more trouble if I got home without my own stuff.

'Quick,' I whispered to Lucy, 'swap back.'

I was now more frightened about the punishment for this than I was about the punishment for running away. We were practically at my house by this time and only had time to change the shoes. I would have to take my chances with the socks.

The moment my mother opened the door she was shouting at me. She didn't seem at all relieved that I was safe, just angry at what I'd done. I was freezing cold and sweating with fear at the same time. When I heard the policeman telling her what Lucy had said about Richard beating me and threatening to kill me, I knew that I was really in trouble.

'Get upstairs to your bedroom,' she shrieked the moment the police had gone, 'and wait there until your dad gets home so he can deal with you.'

He was out, apparently searching for me, and so I got ready for bed with a heavy heart, knowing just what was going to happen once he returned. I couldn't sleep as I lay there listening for the sound of him coming back into the house.

Eventually he was there and I could hear him shouting like a lunatic at Mum and then there was the sound of his feet running up the stairs. His voice was so loud and angry I couldn't make out the words as he ripped the blankets off me and started punching me so hard I thought he was going to kill me. The pain was so bad I actually hoped that this time I would die. In my panic I wet myself and it soaked his arm, making him even angrier and more violent.

I didn't go back to school for about a week after that and was bought lots of new clothes and things, so the bruises must have been pretty bad. They always kept me off school if there was any chance the teachers would see what they'd done to me.

Chapter Two

Torture and cruelty can so easily become routine. Just as Richard could make a joke of pretending to spit in my food to disguise the fact that he was actually doing it, so he could also refer to me, apparently jokingly, as 'Paki slave'. I had to pretend not to mind, otherwise I would have been the one who couldn't take a joke and I would have got a hiding for lacking a sense of humour.

Richard never made any secret of how much he hated all black and Asian people and the fact that I had dark hair and an olive skin that tanned the moment I looked at the sun was enough to categorize me as different and inferior to the rest of the family, someone he could treat in any way he wanted.

He would tell me to sit on the floor in the front room because I was a Paki slave, while they all sat on the comfortable chairs and the sofa. Just as I sat down he would snap his fingers.

'Paki slave, make me and your mum a cup of tea.'

'Paki slave, clean the boots.'

'Paki slave, take the washing out.'

'Paki slave, put the immersion on.'

It would be said as if it were just a game, but I knew I would have to obey the orders with a smile if I didn't want to get a beating for being a bad sport.

By the time I came back into the room with the tea Richard would be giggling with my brothers, encouraging them to snap their fingers like him and send me on another errand. 'Make her do what you want,' he'd tell them, and they would laugh, treating it like the game he was pretending it was. But I had to do what they told me as well, or I would have been accused of not joining in the fun and would have been punished for being a miserable cow.

This 'joke' went on for years. I didn't blame the boys – they didn't know any better and they were as anxious to do as they were told as I was. If the shoe had been on the other foot I expect I would have done the same in order to avoid the beatings. When he was throwing us from wall to wall and punching and kicking us, Richard didn't seem to care what damage he might do. It was as if shutters came down in his brain and he lost all control and reason. No one ever wanted to be on the receiving end of one of those explosions.

At other times, however, he was entirely in control of what he was doing and his malice could not be excused by temper. He used to make me light his cigarettes for him, even when I was small. He got the boys to do it as well, but they just used to lean them on a bar of the electric fire or the top of the cooker until they started to smoulder, whereas I was made to get down and puff to make them light more quickly.

Richard believed that we should be taught how to inhale properly, especially the boys. Sometimes he would make them smoke a whole cigarette, while he and Mum laughed at them and exclaimed how cute they looked as they turned green and coughed as if they were going to choke.

When my brother Dan was two or three they made him light up and suck the smoke in and he started choking and turning red and purple. After a while their laughter turned to panic and they started screaming at him to breathe and banging him on the back. Richard picked him up by the ankles and smacked him like a newborn baby, yelling at me to go and get him some water.

Lighting those cigarettes gave me a taste for smoking by the time I was eleven or twelve, but I knew that if Richard found out I'd taken up the habit he would find some way to turn it into a torture, so I tried to keep it secret for as long as I could.

When I was thirteen I went on a school trip to Belgium that my granddad had paid for. I must have stunk of fags when I got back. The following evening Mum went out to have a cup of tea with a friend across the road, leaving me with Richard.

'You're smoking, aren't you?' he said as soon as we were alone.

'No.' I wondered what was coming next.

'You are,' he said, overruling my protests. 'Here's a fag. You either smoke it or you eat it, unless you tell me the truth.'

I took the cigarette, lit it up and smoked it in front of him.

'Inhale it properly,' he ordered. 'I ain't wasting my money buying you fucking fags if you ain't gonna smoke them properly.'

Once I'd proved to his satisfaction that I was able to smoke properly he gave me a pack of ten, which I took straight up to my bedroom. By the time Mum came back across the road I was leaning out of my bedroom window puffing away happily.

'Alright, Mum?' I said cheerfully.

'What are you doing?' she asked, obviously horrified at the thought of what would happen if Richard saw me.

'I smoke now. It's alright, Dad says I can.'

I guess it didn't bother them because they worked out that if I was a smoker they would soon be able to cadge cigarettes off me when they ran short.

To start with Richard offered me a choice: I could have money for sweets each day or I could have fags. I chose the fags and for the next few mornings there would be a pack of ten waiting for me in a brass horsecart on the mantelpiece. It soon dwindled down to one or two loose ones, which I would use to refill my packet.

There was an awful lot of brass around the house – horse brasses on the wall, brass ornaments on every surface – all of which had to be polished regularly. Mum and Richard did have two big heavy brass soldiers as well, but he got rid of them because Mum kept using them to defend herself when he attacked her.

'You're gonna fucking kill me!' he'd protest whenever she laid into him while fighting back.

As well as cleaning the house from top to bottom several times every day, we had to clean all our boots and shoes, and it had to be done properly, melting the polish into the leather in front of the fire before brushing it in. Everything had to be spotless and shiny, right down to the toilet seat, which was polished so often it was hard not to slide off it. Richard would insist that I made my bed with hospital corners that were exactly ninety degrees. I had no idea what ninety degrees meant, but he still warned me he would be checking them. If ever I complained to Mum, he would tell her he was just joking and that I was a stupid cow to take him seriously, but when we were alone he *was* deadly serious. If I did anything wrong I would be hit or have to pay a penance.

Every little task that he set me I did to the very best of my ability, but it was never enough. If anything, it seemed that the more I tried to please him, the further he wanted to push me, just to show that he could, just to inflict pain, just to show me that I was only allowed to live because he chose not to kill me.

The idea of hurting me must have been playing on his mind all the time, the urge to prove his power over me too delicious to resist. One of his favourite tortures, which started almost as soon as I came home from care, was to suffocate me in bed with my pillow, or with one he brought into the bedroom with him, pressing it down onto my face so hard that I was sure he was sitting on it with all his weight, although he was probably just using his hands. He was very strong when he was excited or angry.

The first few times it happened I was unable to stop myself from screaming as I fought for breath, but I soon learnt that that made it worse because it used what little air there was in my lungs and nobody could hear through the pillow anyway. I would thrash around in my panic, trying to escape, but there was no hope of that happening until he was ready to release me.

When he finally lifted the pillow he would squeeze my face painfully. 'I fucking hate you,' he would say, his face almost touching mine. 'Everyone fucking hates you.' He would then slap me a few times and press the pillow down again.

The only time he would let me get some air was when he thought I was about to pass out. He would check this by lifting my arm and letting it drop, so I learnt to go limp earlier, but he soon cottoned on to that and became angrier still.

I would usually become so frightened under those pillows that I would wet myself, which made him even more incensed, and he would push my face into it like a puppy, rubbing the wet sheet roughly against my skin to teach me a lesson. He'd tell Mum I'd wet the bed, which was why he was angry with me, so she would shout at me too. Sometimes, if she had been out, he would tell her he'd given me a drink which I'd spilled down myself, which would explain why I was in different pyjamas when she came home. That would give him another reason to hit me and shout angrily, and then he would do it all again.

Because the suffocating happened nearly every night I tried different tricks to try to make it better. I would lie on my side when I heard him coming up the stairs, because I found I could breathe more easily that way, and then I decided I could get more air through the mattress than through the pillow, so I would lie on my front, sometimes putting the pillow over my head in readiness for the attack. Richard realized what I was doing quite soon and would put another pillow under my face so that there was no escape. The only thing I could do was stay as still as possible and take shallow breaths. Instinctively I worked out that if I lay quite still it would make it less exciting for him and he was more likely to become bored. I half-hoped that he would succeed in killing me, but he was too cunning for that, always pulling back at the last minute.

It was worse when Mum went out, but sometimes he would even do it when she was downstairs. But there were some tortures, or 'games' as he preferred to call them, which he was happy to inflict on me whoever was around. There were 'thumb jobs', for instance, which entailed him bending my thumb down as far as he could until I was crying out from the pain. That was one he would do for laughs. Another was to make me spread my fingers out on a wooden surface and he would stab a sharp kitchen knife down in between them at faster and faster speeds to show how accurate and fast his reflexes were. Once he carried this further by throwing a paint scraper at my feet so that it sliced between my toes, pinning them to the floor.

If Mum was in the house he might leave me alone after the suffocation game, but if she was out it would just be the start of his night's entertainment.

'Come out here,' he would say once he was bored with the pillow trick, and I would obediently make my way out into the hallway, knowing what was coming.

The ritual was more or less the same each time for many years. He would strip his clothes off and bend over the top few stairs.

'Lick my arse,' he would instruct me and I would reluctantly make my way up to him. I would start by licking his cheeks, hoping he would let me get away with that. That was bad enough, but I always knew it wouldn't be enough for him.

'Lick the hole!' he would snarl at me angrily, and I would have to do it, however sick and humiliated it made me feel. Then he would make me push my finger into it as hard as I could. I guess my finger wasn't big enough to reach wherever he wanted me to reach, though, because then he would often do it to himself.

These nights always had to end with him giving me oral sex and me masturbating him. If Mum was out for the whole night, he would keep the 'games' going for hours. Sometimes he would want me to smack his bum and tell him he was a naughty boy. Sometimes he would make me go on all fours, with my arms and legs straight, and he would rub his penis around my back and front entrances, pushing into my back entrance.

The force of his weight would make me move away even if I tried not to, which wasn't what he wanted, so he would take me downstairs to the sofa so I couldn't move. At other times he would lay me across his lap with my knickers down, or off completely, and smack, bite, kiss or play with my bottom and my vagina.

'I can't stand to look at your fucking ugly face!' he'd tell me, and I would have to kneel with my face pressed against his bottom and put my arm through his legs to masturbate him. Or he would sit me on his lap and wriggle me around, telling me to keep the movements going myself.

When he was performing oral sex on me I would try to disconnect myself from my body, distracting my mind by counting things like the patterns on the wallpaper or the digits on the clock counter on the video. If the television was on I would close my eyes and spell out the things that people were saying and count the letters in my head, anything to keep my mind busy so that I didn't have to think about what he was doing to me. Sometimes he would shout at me to move my bottom up and down or to pull his hair while he was doing it and masturbating himself.

If my brothers were upstairs in their bedrooms, they knew better than to come out for any reason. God knows how much they heard or understood of the night-time noises outside their closed doors.

Although Richard fought with everyone he came into contact with, bullying everyone, regardless of their age or gender, I don't think there was anyone else that he degraded sexually in the way that he degraded me. Everyone in the area hated him, though, and they didn't much like the way my mum carried on either. All day long I would be sent out to knock on doors and cadge cigarettes, teabags, washing powder or anything else that she needed and couldn't be bothered to go out and buy for herself.

The neighbours must have been able to watch me going from door to door. I bet sometimes they would avoid answering my knock. 'Oh, Janey,' they would say in despairing voices when I came back with my fifth request of the day. They all knew they would never be paid back for anything that was borrowed.

Although they spent a fortune doing up their houses, Mum and Richard never had enough money for the essentials of life. Mum would always buy a cheap toilet roll on a Monday when she got her giro cheque, but with seven people in the house it was gone by Tuesday and we would be using torn up newspapers for the rest of the week. I got into the habit of filling my pockets with tissues wherever I came across them. I stole a toilet roll from school once and Mum told me to get more, but I made up some excuse as to why I couldn't. Every time I went out of the house Mum would say, 'Try and get some toilet roll.' I couldn't understand how she and Richard could afford to smoke and eat McDonald's, Chinese and curries, but not to buy the basic decencies of life.

Sometimes if Mum had run out of cigarettes and the giro wasn't due I would have to go out with one of my little brothers and scour the streets for dog-ends, so she could take the tobacco out and make roll ups. I had to keep it a secret from Richard, because he would have gone mad if he'd known we were showing ourselves up like that. I was so ashamed I would tell my friends we were looking for stones, but they knew perfectly well what we were doing. They were always very kind to me. I think they felt sorry for me, having to live with Richard.

Everyone was meant to believe that Richard didn't work, which he didn't for years. Then he started doing shifts as a mini-cab driver, but didn't want to give up the disability benefit he received for his 'bad leg', so the work had to be kept quiet. He would unscrew the aerial from the roof of the car whenever he came home and cover up the two-way radio. He would even use a walking stick sometimes, particularly if he'd noticed a new car in the street and thought social services were spying on him. If they had spied on him they would have been able to see him building sheds, laying patios and doing up houses with no trouble at all, not to mention beating people up when they annoyed him.

We were always under strict instructions to lie to anyone who asked about him and to act as if he were really poorly. My friends would always tell me that everyone knew what he was up to, but no one wanted to accuse him to his face.

He even went to the trouble of having handrails fitted in the bathroom so that he could claim a higher level of welfare payment. 'I hate having those fucking ugly things in my house,' he would complain, but he was happy to do anything that would bring in a bit more easy money.

I would have to make plenty of trips to the shops as well as to neighbours' houses during the average day, always sent on the spur of the moment and my journey timed to make sure I didn't take any detours and meet up with a friend or play with the other kids who messed about in the car park which was a couple of doors away.

Sometimes, however, things would go wrong. One day, for instance, when I was still small, I was sent to get Richard some cigarettes and a few other things.

'Don't be long,' he warned, and I could see he was in a bad mood.

I hurried down the road and got to the shop in record time, but the people behind the counter wouldn't sell me cigarettes and so I knew I was going to have to stand outside as usual asking other customers to buy them for me. That could sometimes take ages, as most people would refuse. This particular day it took what seemed like hours and I was becoming increasingly agitated. If I went back without them I would be in trouble, but if I took too long Richard would think I'd gone to play with a friend, disobeying his orders. It looked as if there was going to be no way out of getting a smack at the very least.

Eventually a man came along who lived opposite us and I begged him to help me, promising that I was buying the cigarettes for my parents. He seemed to believe me, got the cigarettes for me and then asked if I wanted a lift home. We'd been told never to accept lifts from strange men, but I often played with this man's daughters and knew his wife. There didn't seem to be any danger and I was eager to get back as quickly as possible in the hope of avoiding a punishment, so I accepted his offer, assuming he would park in the car park round the corner and my stepfather wouldn't see me getting out of the car. To my horror, however, the neighbour, presumably thinking he was doing me a favour, dropped me off right outside the house. As I came in through the front door Richard went berserk, shouting and screaming, hitting me around the head and kicking me.

'I'm sorry, I'm sorry,' I kept saying over and over again, but I couldn't make him stop.

'Stand against the backroom window,' he ordered, 'and put your arms down by your sides.'

There was no one else in the house to intervene. I did as he told me, terrified of what new torture he might have thought up but equally terrified of moving and angering him still further. So when he pulled back his fist I didn't flinch, taking the punch full in the face.

'You deserve that,' he shouted, finally happy that he had taught me a lesson. 'Never get in anyone's car again.'

As the boys grew older my duties towards them increased. I didn't mind that too much because I loved them when they were little and they were very affectionate back. The younger ones used to call me 'Mum' a lot of the time, which would make me laugh. I liked it when they did that; it made me feel they were grateful for what I did for them.

Richard kept wanting more children because he was trying to have a girl of his own. Even when Mum got ill and lost a kidney, he insisted that they went on trying.

Mum and Richard would stay in bed in the mornings once I was able to get the others up and sort out their breakfasts. I was always turning up at school with safety pins all over my clothes from changing nappies.

If the boys woke up early they would come into my room. All of us were terrified of making a noise and disturbing the sleeping adults. To entertain them and keep them quiet until it was time for breakfast I would sit them in a line and dress them up in my clothes, doing their hair as if they were my dolls. They loved it, but when Richard found out he went mad, saying I was trying to turn them into 'poofs'.

If Mum got up, Silly Git would stay in bed and I would be sent up to give him cups of tea. On each trip I would have to do him some horrible little 'favour'. He would make me come right up to the edge of the bed, lifting up my skirt and tugging my knickers down so that he could touch me. I would then have to play with him under the covers for a few minutes until Mum called me back downstairs again.

'Bring me up a fag,' he would say as I went out the door, and the same thing would happen again when I returned. He always insisted on having two cups of tea before he got up, both brought to him by me.

As the years went by we all used to confide in one another how much we hated Richard, but never when he was in earshot. Mum used to tell us how she was just waiting until the boys had finished school and then we would all be off. Sometimes, when he had given her a beating, she would tell me that once the boys were grown up they would all turn on him for her.

On a few occasions Mum did pluck up the courage to leave him, with all of us walking along behind her like a parade of baby ducks. But he always did whatever was necessary to drag her back, regardless of who might be watching.

On one occasion he was driving his car when he came for her, winding the window down and driving slowly along beside her as she looked straight ahead and pretended not to see him.

'Get in the fucking car!' he ordered.

'Fuck off!' she replied.

Without another word he reached out of the window and grabbed her hair, then reversed the car back up to the house, literally dragging her back by the hair, not caring about the danger or who might see.

Sometimes he would playact being pathetic and unable to remember whether he had taken his tablets. He took them for the pains in his legs, something to do with trapped nerves, although no one ever really got to the bottom of it. He used to go to pain clinic and I had to go with him once to learn how to give him acupuncture, sticking needles in his back. Richard knew I was too frightened to be tempted to do him any damage with the needles.

Being in pain often made him moody.

'Have I taken my tablets?' he would whine.

'No,' one of us would lie, 'I don't think you have.'

'You give them to him,' Mum would whisper to me if we were in another room. 'Maybe they'll finish him off.'

'No,' I would hiss back, 'you do it!'

But he would only be pretending. Whenever one or other of us plucked up the courage to take the potential overdose out to him, he would look pensive. 'You know,' he would say, as if the thought was just occurring to him, 'I think I did take them.'

Richard seemed to actually get a kick out of fighting people, whether they were relatives, neighbours or just strangers on the street. There was never any logic to why he would decide to pick on them – he would just trump up some reason from nowhere to justify spreading his hatred around and demonstrating his superior strength. He had enemies everywhere, but only occasionally would they be brave enough to retaliate.

One Sunday evening, when my brothers and I were about to get into the bath and we were naked at the top of the stairs, bricks started crashing through the glass in the front door.

'Stay there!' Mum shouted as we began screaming, and she ran downstairs. Silly Git was arming himself with a thick rusty chain and we watched as he ran outside barefoot to face the men who were waiting in the car park for him. There were about eight of them and some of them had machetes and similar weapons. Mum ran outside after him, screaming and waving a carving knife. Family honour, it seemed, was at stake here.

We stood at the window and watched them fighting until the police came to take them all away. It was like watching the Incredible Hulk at work. Richard was angry and when that happened he didn't care who he took on or how bad the odds were. Displays like that made me all the more certain that he was capable of killing me and Mum if I ever disobeyed him.

He enjoyed making the rest of us fight as well, seeing it as a badge of honour for the family if we pulped someone else's face. If Mum had made friends with another woman in the street he would tell her that she had been badmouthing her and would send her round to sort her out. I'm sure Mum must have known he was making it up, but she pretended to believe him in order to avoid a beating herself, I guess, and would go round to the woman's house and beat her up instead.

Although Mum made it clear to me that she hated living with Richard, she seemed to have the same delusions about the need to be violent as he did. One day a boy from across the street got me in the eye with a pellet from a potato gun. I thought I was blinded and ran into the house crying. Mum sent me straight out to hit him back and show him the error of his ways. Knowing that I would be in big trouble if I lost the fight, I did as I was told and unleashed all the pent-up anger I could find, spurred on by the pain in my eye. The poor boy didn't know what had hit him, and even though he was a pretty tough kid himself, his mum had to come running out of the house to separate us.

'Your Janey's a bleeding lunatic,' another neighbour told Mum admiringly, which Mum seemed to take as a fine compliment. I felt proud of myself for upholding the family honour and doing my duty.

One summer holiday my cousin Tracy came to stay with us for a few weeks. I was so excited when I heard because no one ever came to stay with us and it would mean I had a girl I could play with instead of just my brothers. It also meant she would be staying in my room, which might mean Silly Git would have fewer opportunities to do things to me.

Although he still found ways of getting at me, even with Tracy there, she did obviously make it harder for him and he started to resent her presence around the house quite soon after she arrived. He began being unpleasant to her in the hope that she'd ask to go home, but she seemed not to take any notice, having no idea just how dangerous he was when he didn't get things his own way.

One afternoon we were all playing in the garden and Richard and Mum were sitting on the patio watching us and drinking tea. Tracy and I were doing handstands on the grass and my brothers were running races. Silly Git must have been feeling left out and bored, or maybe plain mischievous. He wouldn't have liked seeing me having fun like a normal little girl, not unless my happiness put me in his debt in some way.

'Jane,' he shouted. 'Get over here.'

Tracy trotted innocently over with me.

'Fuck off, Nosey,' he snarled at her. 'I weren't calling you!'

Once she was out of earshot he beckoned me closer. 'That Tracy's being nasty to your brother,' he told me. I knew it wasn't true, but there was nothing I could say so I just looked at him, waiting to hear what would come next. 'So what are you going to fucking do about it?'

'Tracy and me were playing handstands,' I said, trying not to sound as if I was arguing, a sick feeling of foreboding building in my stomach. 'The boys were playing on their own.'

'Don't argue,' he shouted. 'You just go and hit her. Stick up for your brother.'

'I don't want to,' I protested, knowing as I spoke that it was pointless to say anything now that he was getting angry.

'We're a fucking family,' he snarled. 'We fucking stick up for each other. You show some fucking loyalty and hit her for what she's done to your brother.'

Not only did I not want to hit Tracy because she was my cousin and my friend, but she was also a lot bigger than me and would beat me up. I didn't mind that so much, but I knew that if I lost the fight Richard would punish me later for letting the family down. We were all supposed to be these hard people who never let anyone take any liberties with us. It was a question of pride or something.

I tried pleading once more. It was no use. 'Just fucking get on with it,' he instructed and I knew there was no getting out of it.

I went back to Tracy with a heavy heart. 'What did you be nasty to Tom for?' I asked.

She looked puzzled.

'Go on then!' my stepfather shouted from the patio, impatient for the fight to begin.

'I'm sorry,' I whispered and gave her a gentle push.

Confused by all the shouting and the sudden end to our game, Tracy pushed me back and a few seconds later we were rolling on the floor punching, scratching, pinching and pulling hair. My stepfather was cheering me on from the sidelines like a proud parent watching their kid performing in a school match. It wasn't long before Tracy had managed to pin me to the floor and was laying into me with quite justifiable anger. There was hair everywhere and our faces were covered in deep scratches. We were both crying because of the pain we were inflicting on one another and because we'd been having such a good time a few minutes before and now it was all spoiled. My stepdad was becoming furious with me for losing and letting the family down, screaming at me to beat Tracy up, but she was too strong for me and I didn't want to hurt her any more anyway.

Both of us had tired ourselves out, but Richard hadn't seen nearly enough sport yet. He dragged Tracy off me, grabbing both our collars and hauling us inside the house, excited by the fighting, furious that his fighter was losing and determined to get revenge on Tracy. He pulled us roughly up the stairs and into one of the bedrooms, pushing two of my brothers' beds apart to make a boxing ring.

'Now you're fucking gonna do it properly,' he ordered. I knew he meant we had to box and kick and abide by rules he laid down, two little bare-knuckle fighters. There was to be no more girlie hair-pulling or scratching. And this time he knew I would win, because he'd trained me, along with my brothers, in how to box.

We started out by hitting each other softly, but Richard knew we were pulling our punches and shouted that I'd get a good hiding from him if I didn't get on with it and beat her up, so I started fighting for real because I was far more scared of him than I was of poor Tracy. We fought for him like pit-bull terriers for what seemed like ages before Mum couldn't take it any more and split us up.

Tracy was sent home after that. She got such a telling off for the 'trouble she'd caused', but there was nothing I could do about it. Maybe my stepfather was jealous, wanting to have his family all to himself and to exclude any outsider who didn't understand that he was to be feared and obeyed without question. Eventually he fell out with Tracy's parents and they steered clear of us for years, just like everyone else.

Richard used to like to make us fight each other as well, even when the boys were tiny. If we were arguing about something, as brothers and sisters always do, he'd order us to fight it out properly. I was made to kneel down, because I was so much taller than them, and I wasn't allowed to scratch, but those were the only rules.

I didn't want to hit the boys, because I loved them and they were just little kids, but Richard would make us punch each other as hard as we could. We could also pull hair, bite and strangle one another, but the boys always had shaved heads so I had nothing to get hold of. We'd all be in tears because we didn't want to do it, tufts of my hair would be pulled out and there would be blood and bruises on all of us. Although I would try not to hurt my brothers, they would be forced to hurt me and sometimes I would lash out automatically because I'd been punched in the face or one of them had his hands tight round my throat. If I did as I was told and really punched one of them in the hope of ending the fight quickly, I'd be hauled off and punished for being too violent with someone so small. There was no way we could win and we would always end up sobbing and miserable. At times like that I knew the boys hated their father as much as I did.

Although I didn't mind looking after my little brothers, I was too young to be left in charge of them and it was inevitable that something terrible would happen. I was trying to get the three big ones ready for school one morning and changing Les's nappy at the same time. I was making them toast under the grill, doing up their shoes, finding their clothes as they got dressed in front of the fire and getting myself ready, and I took my eye off little Les for just a second. He was one year old at the time, but big for his age. He had weighed a stone when he was born and had kept growing after that. Impatient to get his morning drink, he must have reached up and tugged the flex of the kettle while I was looking the other way, and he pulled the whole thing down on top of him. The boiling water made his skin bubble and blister, and the screaming was terrible. He was in hospital for three months and the scars on his arms never went, although his face healed eventually.

I was never allowed to forget that it was me who did that to him, scarring him for life.

'Who burnt you, Les?' Silly Git would ask him every so often.

'Janey done it,' he would reply dutifully. 'Janey burnt me.'

I was twelve at the time.

Chapter Three

My favourite person was always my granddad, Mum's dad. He wasn't that old and everyone seemed to like him. He was dark-haired and skinned, like an Italian. I guess I got my colouring from him. When he was young he used to dress like a Teddy boy, with the DA haircut. He worked as a driver for someone very senior in business and had two huge American cars, an orange one and a white one, and two Yorkshire terriers. I thought of them as a little married couple, especially as the boy had what looked like a little beard. I used to love tying ribbons in their hair and dressing them up in dark glasses and anything else I could persuade them to wear, just as I had with my brothers when they were small. The dogs never complained; they were happy to have any sort of attention.

Knowing how much I liked dogs, Granddad brought us a black Labrador. The man he worked for had some connection with the royal family and this dog was from the same family as the Queen's gun dogs. He was a lovely animal, but Silly Git found a black hair on his dinner plate one day and he had to go. He took him out into the country somewhere and tied him to a tree. Someone helpful brought him back, so he had to do it again.

This wasn't the first dog we'd had, or the first to disappear. There had been a mongrel in the house when I was small. He used to knock on the door when he wanted to be let in and would go down the shops with me whenever I was sent on errands. But when I came home from school one day I was told he'd been run over and killed. Maybe he had. I never found out.

Granddad used to take me shopping at Tesco with him in his flash cars so we could pose. Everyone would stop and watch as we cruised past, him with his sunglasses on and me feeling like a princess, snuggled up beside him because there were no gear sticks or handbrakes in the way. Inside the shop he would do things that would make me laugh, like taking his false teeth out and putting them on the conveyor belt when we got to the tills, or climbing up one of the stepladders they used for filling the top shelves and singing a song to the assembled shoppers below. I would be cringing with embarrassment but loving it at the same time. If I asked to go shopping with Granddad, Richard and Mum would instruct me to tell him I needed a new coat or new plimsolls. I hated having to ask, but I think he knew I had to. He nearly always got me what I asked for, if he could.

At one stage he used to live next door to us with his youngest son, my uncle John, who was only four years older than me and more like a brother than an uncle. Granddad used to collect all sorts of things, including birds like quails and pigeons, which he used to keep in an aviary at the bottom of his garden, and fish, which lived in a huge pond with a bridge across it. If we were out in the garden we would call to him through the fence, 'Granddad! Granddad! Can we have some chocolate, Granddad?' and he'd haul himself out of the hammock where he had been lying and would push miniature Mars bars through the holes in the chain-link fence.

I don't remember my nan, but I do remember the wooden box she had left with all her jewellery in it. Granddad must have had some money at one time because there was a Rolex watch in there and an eighteen-carat gold charm bracelet. Each charm represented a significant event in Nan's life. For instance, there was a tiny cathedral which you could open up, which he had given her when they got married, and there were also her engagement and eternity rings. The bracelet was a huge great thing, much too heavy to wear. Granddad gave the box to me, but inevitably Richard and Mum sold the watch to pay for something or other and pawned the bracelet. They promised me they would redeem it for me, but of course they never did. That was my nan's whole life gone and I felt so sad.

When I got a bit older Granddad used to pay me to do his housework. He would write me out cheques for three pounds, which made me feel really rich. One day he asked me to make him a fresh cup of tea.

'Oh, Granddad,' I complained. 'I just made you one.'

'Go on,' he cajoled, 'and rinse this cup out well first.'

When I took the cup to the sink and poured away the dregs, a gold bracelet plopped out. I knew to keep this one secret.

Granddad had a big gold ring in the house too, which was studded with rubies. He knew I loved it.

'You can't have that,' he said, 'because your Mum will just sell it. But you can wear it while you do the housework if you like.'

He had a brother living in Australia and he was always planning to go and visit him, touring the world on the way there and back. He offered to take me with him. Silly Git refused, saying that it wasn't fair on the boys.

'I can't take them all,' Granddad protested, 'and it will be a chance in a lifetime for her.' But nothing was going to change my stepfather's mind.

One year, though, Granddad was actually allowed to take me away on holiday. We went to Hastings in the tourer caravan that he kept on the drive and it was just him, me and the dogs. It was like heaven, feeling safe and happy all the time.

Granddad also had a static caravan in a holiday park at Southend. We sometimes went there as a family at weekends or during the holidays, and if Granddad was around it was harder for Richard to get at me. He still managed to, of course. In the evening he would tell the others to go out to bingo, offering to stay in with me because I'd been naughty earlier in the day and had to be punished.

'Oh, Janey,' Mum would sigh, 'what have you done now?'

'We've been in a caravan together all day,' I'd think. 'You know everything I've done.' But I never said anything in my own defence, knowing that would ignite Richard's wrath, and Mum would be willing to accept that I needed to be punished. So they would all go off without me, leaving me alone with Richard for a few hours. I usually got to go out one evening in every holiday, but to earn that treat I would have to go out for a walk with him earlier in the day to find a quiet place where I could 'do him a favour'.

One year he actually announced that he was going to go home for the day to collect a giro, because otherwise we wouldn't have any cash. Needless to say I had to go with him. He would always use the same excuse: 'I'll take Jane with me in case my leg plays up. She can make me my tea and get me my fags.' That was always the reason why I had to be with him wherever he went. This time I couldn't believe that not only was I going to have to spend an uninterrupted night with him but I was going to be missing my holiday as well.

When we got home we had to go straight to his and Mum's bed, where he spent hours abusing me. It was awful knowing that no one was going to be coming back and there was nothing I could do to stop him. Once it was all over he went to sleep cuddling me as if I was his wife and in the morning we had to do the whole thing all over again.

If ever Mum was away for the night, which was quite often when she got ill with her kidneys or when she was away giving birth, I would have to sleep in the bed with Richard as if we were a couple and one morning one of my brothers saw me coming out, even though I always tried to get back to my own bed before they woke up.

'What you doing in there?' he wanted to know. I made up some excuse about having gone in there to get something and he seemed to accept my explanation without question, but then why wouldn't he? What child could have imagined what was going on between his father and his sister?

One of my uncles had a caravan, too, just in front of Granddad's, and we would go there as well, but when it was just Granddad and me it was the best time imaginable, whether we were in the caravan or out shopping or in his house.

It couldn't last, of course, because nothing good ever did. Richard took against Granddad and Uncle John, just as he took against everyone. He did everything he could to stop me going round to their house because he knew how much I enjoyed it and how kind Granddad was to me. I guess he was afraid I'd let something slip if I was there too much.

Once Richard had taken against someone his vindictiveness would be irrational and petty. One moment he would be attacking my uncle in the street, the next he would be sneaking around the back, cutting through their television aerial and telephone wires.

Because I knew my way around Granddad's house Richard used to lift me over the fence when he was out and make me break in and take things that he and Mum wanted, like food or tobacco or something from the freezer. Sometimes it would just be money or a credit card that they were after because they wanted to go shopping. I hated doing it because it made me feel that I was betraying Granddad.

When Uncle John eventually married, Richard took against his poor wife and if he saw her in the street he would try to run her over.

Granddad also had a girlfriend he was planning to marry, but Mum and Richard took against her for no reason other than she wasn't 'family'. If we happened to come out of our house at the same time as Granddad, I was instructed to ignore him, and I would never have dared to disobey such a direct order. I was later told that that nearly broke his heart. They eventually beat him up and drove him and my uncle away. I think there was a final argument over some money they'd borrowed off him or something, but the reasons didn't mean anything, they had just decided to drive him away. By that time Granddad had had a stroke and Mum and Richard were worried that he would die and they wouldn't inherit a share of his house because he would leave it to his widow.

People sometimes used to complain to the police after they'd been attacked or intimidated by my stepdad, but they always withdrew the charges after receiving a warning visit from Richard or Mum. They all decided it was easier to get the council to move them to another estate than to face the intimidation and violence that went with trying to get justice. So there was no one to stop him doing whatever he wanted, whenever he wanted. To me, as a child, he seemed invincible. There was no point trying to fight him or escape from his power, because he would always win in the end and the retribution would always be worse than whatever had come before. So whenever I was asked to do something, no matter how petty or obscene it might be, I knew I had to agree with a merry laugh if I didn't want a beating or worse.

As I grew older he would make me do him different favours. Sometimes he would drop a favourite routine for a while and try something new, occasionally going back to an old practice for a change. I never knew when some new demand was going to be made.

One summer's day we were all outside cleaning the car in front of the house and doing some gardening when Richard suddenly went inside with no explanation. I didn't think anything of it until he leant out of the open bedroom window and called down to me to come up and help him out with something. My heart sank, but I told myself it couldn't be anything too terrible because Mum and the boys were all around. I didn't even bother to close the front door as I went in, thinking I would be going back out again in a few minutes.

When I got to the bedroom he was standing waiting for me.

'Shut the door,' he said.

I obeyed.

'You've been bad,' he went on.

My heart sank. I knew I was in trouble.

'You're in my little black book.'

I'd never heard of this little black book before.

'You know what for, don't you?'

'Yes,' I lied, knowing that if I protested my innocence or ignorance he'd hit me for being cheeky or for lying.

'You'll have to be punished for being in the black book.'

I nodded, having no idea what he was planning but certain it would be unpleasant.

He made me kneel down in front of him and unzipped his trousers. Even though I'd never done it before, I suddenly knew what was coming next.

'Put it in your mouth,' he said, 'and suck it nicely.'

The window was still open, the net curtains blowing in the breeze, and I could hear Mum outside telling the boys to keep cleaning the car and not to go inside the house. Maybe it was because they were wet and would make a mess on the carpets, or maybe it was because she didn't want them stumbling across something they shouldn't see. I was terrified they would come in and find us and Richard would be sent into a rage and would attack Mum and it would all be my fault. It was making me feel sick and I started crying, which made him angry.

'Do it properly,' he ordered, pushing my head towards him, making me gag but giving me no chance to disengage.

When I'd done it enough he took it out of my mouth and masturbated himself in front of me. We then went back downstairs to rejoin the others and continue cleaning the car as if we were one big happy family.

The sexual abuse itself was never enough for him, he always had to wrap it up in some sort of psychological torture which he would pretend was a game that we were both enjoying.

One day, for instance, when everyone else was out, he called me to the top of the stairs.

'You owe me a favour,' he told me. 'So you can have a choice of how to repay me.'

The choice, it seemed, was him giving me oral sex, me doing it for him or me kissing him on the lips. I'd never had to kiss him before and I thought that would be the least disgusting of the three options. At least he wouldn't be touching me anywhere private.

Once I had chosen the kiss he told me that I was going to have to put my tongue in his mouth. I thought I was going to die. I tried to do it so he wouldn't become angry, but it just made me gag. Because it was so disgusting, even worse than the oral sex, I couldn't do it properly and he became furious, making me do all three things as a punishment for doing it badly.

Thinking about it afterwards, I realized it had been a trick all along and that he had always intended to make me do everything. Any 'games' involving 'choices' were just that, games. I would always be the loser, so in the future I might as well choose the worst option first in the hope of getting it over and done with as quickly as possible.

When you're a small child you sort of assume that your life is normal, that everyone else is going through much the same experiences as you are. The first indication I had that perhaps this wasn't so was when I was out playing with one of my friends and she said she was going to go home.

'But your mum's out,' I said, genuinely surprised by her decision.

'It's okay, my dad's there,' she replied, as if it were the most natural thing in the world, and I realized that she wasn't actually frightened of being in the house on her own with her father. Was it possible that her dad never hurt her? Was I the only one who was being made to do these things? How could I find out when I had been told that Mum and I would be killed if I ever discussed such private matters with anyone else?

Eventually I mustered the courage to confide what was happening to me to my friend Hayley, having absolutely sworn her to secrecy and extracted a secret from her first in order to secure her discretion.

At first she couldn't understand what I was trying to tell her.

'You know,' I said when she looked puzzled, 'he makes me do the sort of things that married couples do.'

She was horrified and immediately wanted to tell her mum so that he could be stopped. I reminded her of her vow and of the secret I was holding of hers. I warned her I would have to kill myself if she breathed a word and she saw that I was serious. She thought for a while.

'As he's not your real dad,' she suggested eventually, 'perhaps you could just pretend you're having an affair.'

'I don't want to have an affair with him!' I wailed and from the look on her face I think she was able to understand my pain, even if she wasn't completely able to understand what was happening to me, and knew that she could never breathe a word until I was ready. She was the best friend I could possibly have asked for. But even though I knew I could trust her, I still had rushes of panic when I thought about what would happen if she ever let my secret slip out.

The next time Silly Git asked me to do something horrible I plucked up all my courage and complained that Hayley didn't have to do that sort of thing for her dad.

'How do you know?' he demanded, instantly suspicious.

'I don't know,' I backtracked quickly, knowing how terrible the retribution would be if he thought I'd told anyone about what happened between us. 'I can just tell she doesn't.'

'You ever tell her anything and I'll kill you,' he promised, and I had no reason to doubt it.

Hayley and I were as inseparable as we could be, considering how little I was allowed out of the house. Whenever I was given permission we used to play rounders or skate in the car park round the corner or sit playing cards in the tourer caravan that Granddad kept parked in his drive. Even then, however, my freedom had limits. When the other kids got tired of staying in the car park and wanted to go round the block, Hayley would always stay with me, knowing I wasn't allowed to go any further from the house. Sometimes, if Richard was off mini-cabbing for a few hours and Hayley's mum was in with my mum, she would plead, 'Oh, let her go with the others,' and Mum wouldn't be able to think up any reason why I shouldn't be treated just like them, so I was allowed to go, but this didn't happen often.

Knowing that she couldn't come knocking on my door and that most of the time I was forbidden to knock on hers, Hayley used to sit on a wall just out of sight of our windows, waiting for me to come past on one of my dozens of trips to the shop every day. She never had long to wait and we would chatter all the way there and back, with her peeling off at the last corner so that Mum and Richard wouldn't see us together and think I'd disobeyed orders and knocked for her as I'd passed. We became 'blood sisters' on the grass outside a block of flats in our street, picking scabs off our knees and rubbing them together so our blood would mingle. She would eventually prove to be as true and faithful as any blood sister could be, putting herself and her family in considerable danger in order to speak up for me.

Hayley's mum was pretty friendly with mine and one evening when my stepdad was off mini-cabbing, she came over to our house for a smoke and a chat and they sent me back to Hayley's house to babysit her little brother and sister with her. Once the little children were in bed, we decided to raid the drinks cupboard and found her mum's bottle of Malibu, plus a few others, and pretended to each other that we were getting roaring drunk as we took swigs from each bottle.

When Hayley's mum returned unexpectedly and said I had to go back because my dad had come home early, I felt sick with fear in case he worked out what I'd been up to. I had no idea I had actually become drunk until my head hit the fresh air and I tried to get back across the road to our house and found myself ricocheting off every car in the street.

Part of my brain was sober enough to know that if Richard realized I was drunk I would be in big trouble. I made a huge effort to make my movements and voice seem normal. Before going into the house I took a deep breath and tried to compose myself, but all that happened was that a terrible urge rose inside me to giggle, which I knew would earn me a good beating because my stepdad wouldn't be able to understand what I was laughing at. I took a few more seconds and then let myself into the house. I took off my shoes and socks so that I didn't make any marks or leave any fluff on the carpet and popped my head round the door to the front room to see what the mood was like.

Richard and Mum were both there and Richard was sitting in his armchair eating the four egg mayo sandwiches that Mum always packed in his lunchbox when he worked nights, ready for him when he came home. It was a large lunchbox and I could see it quite clearly as I walked into the room. It was on the floor and there was plenty of space to walk round it, but for some reason my bare feet weren't obeying my brain. It was as if they were being pulled by a magnet towards those soft moist sandwiches. I stood frozen in fear as I felt them squelch beneath my toes, waiting for the explosion.

'You been drinking?' they both asked, laughing.

For some reason I didn't get into any trouble, just had to peel the sandwiches off the soles of my feet and go to bed. The next morning they made me apologize to Hayley's mum for stealing her drink. She thought it was all a big laugh.

It was strange how sometimes things that I would have thought would get me in trouble were no problem at all. It was as if all the normal rules of good parenting had been turned on their heads. It was always impossible to tell when Mum and Richard would find something funny and allow me to laugh too. It was as if I needed to have their permission to laugh and if I did it without permission they would think I was being cheeky or laughing at them and I would get a wallop. It was all very confusing.

One of Richard's favourite places to take me was the loft. There was no ladder, which made it difficult to get to and unlikely that my mother or anyone else would disturb us without us hearing them coming. There were no lights either, and no boards on the floor, just a few bits of wood at one end.

Richard would tell Mum we were going up to look for something or other, climbing up from the banister and pulling me up after him, lighting a candle or matches and making a few rustling noises to let her think he was searching for something. When we got to the far end he would get out some pornographic magazines and look at them while stroking my chest and private parts and making me masturbate him. If Mum disturbed us by shouting up to find out what was keeping us, or if I hadn't done a good enough job, or if I had a miserable expression on my face, he would blow out the candle and leave me up there on my own, telling

Mum I was being moody or sulky and needed to be taught a lesson.

I hated it up there in the dark amidst the spiders and God knows what else. I would sit at the edge of the hatch looking down at what seemed an impossibly long drop.

'If you want to get down, then jump,' Richard would taunt, 'or else you can stay up there all fucking day!'

He would eventually get me down because Mum would start moaning at him.

Sometimes when Mum had gone out to bingo and he knew she was going to be some time, he would bring the magazines downstairs and make me re-enact what the women in the pictures were doing and read out loud the words that were written in the bubbles coming out of their mouths. He would get cross if I did it wrong. If the boys were in the house they knew better than to come out of their rooms once they'd been sent to bed.

One day Mum went up to the loft herself when Richard was out mini-cabbing and she needed some clothes. I begged her not to, but couldn't give her any good reason why not. I stood helplessly on the landing as she fetched a chair and hoisted herself up. I could see through the hatch that she was rooting around in the area where he kept the magazines. As she came back down onto the chair she had them in her hand. She asked me what they were doing up there and I could feel myself turning bright red with shame.

'I don't know,' I muttered guiltily.

What made her think that I knew anything about them? Why would she imagine that a little girl would be storing pornography in the loft, unless she suspected the truth?

When Richard got home she showed him the magazines. 'Look what that dirty bastard left in the loft when he moved out,' she said, referring to the previous owner of the house. 'I knew there was something dodgy about him.'

'Disgusting,' Richard agreed. 'I wouldn't want anything to do with filth like that.'

I have no idea if Mum believed him or not, but it certainly wouldn't have been a good idea for her to express any doubts if she had them.

Life continued as if nothing had happened.

Chapter Four

I always wanted to believe that Mum knew nothing about what was going on. No child wants to believe that their mother knows they are suffering and chooses to do nothing about it. Because I knew how much she suffered at Richard's hands as well, I put her on a pedestal and was always determined to protect her if ever I could. I believed that if I let her know what was going on, I would be putting both our lives in danger. I would never forget the feel of that carving knife on my throat and I never doubted for a moment that Richard was capable of carrying out his threat to murder her if I said anything.

When I got older Mum and I used to go out shopping together, giggling all the time, and she liked to believe that people were looking at us and thinking we were sisters. Although she let me down a lot by not protecting me from Richard when she could have done, I still thought the world of her. One of the bonds between us was woven from my knowledge of what he did to her.

Once, when I was about ten, Mum's screams woke me up in the middle of the night. I knew that meant Richard was hitting her as usual, but this time the noises coming from the bedroom next door sounded especially loud. I was shaking and telling myself to just stay calm and it would soon all be over, it always was. I knew that if I went in he would turn his fury onto me for interfering and it wouldn't make anything better for her. Now he was shouting at the top of his voice and there was a repeated banging noise, which sounded like her head being smashed against the adjoining wall. I was terrified that this time he really would kill her and then I would be left alone with him. As I lay there, praying she wouldn't die, the screams stopped but the banging continued. I could hear the boys crying in their beds, too frightened to move. Mum was making a groaning noise, 'Huh, huh.'

Fear giving me courage, I climbed out of bed and ran out onto the landing, pushing open their bedroom door. The light from the hallway illuminated the sight of my mother on all fours, wearing nothing but her knickers, while Richard stood astride her, pulling her head back by the hair, his other hand under her chin, about to smash her head against the wall again. They both froze and looked at me.

'Leave her alone!' I screamed.

'Go back to bed,' Mum whispered.

Richard looked at me for a second longer, then let my mother's limp body drop onto the floor and started running out after me. I managed to get into my room and slam my door, but by the time I reached my bed he'd burst through and caught up with me, shouting, punching and throwing me around. It was one of the worst beatings I'd ever endured.

Then I heard Mum's voice coming from behind him. 'Get off her,' she said, and it sounded as though she meant it.

I looked up and saw her standing behind him, holding the carving knife that she always kept under her mattress. She looked as though she was hyperventilating as she panted and shook with a mixture of pain, fear and rage.

Richard stopped beating me, threw me down on the bed, straightened up and walked out of the room, still shouting abuse.

Mum came in and sat on the bed, laying me across her lap and rubbing my back to comfort me. I must have been winded because I was having trouble getting my breath. I kept watching the door, knowing he would be back, that he wouldn't be able to let her have the last word like that.

A few minutes later he was there again, exploding into the room, picking up my chest of drawers and hurling it at us. It hit me full in the back, knocking me off Mum's lap, and she leapt up, screaming, the carving knife back in her hand, and stabbed him in the side of his stomach.

I curled up into a ball by the bed, trying to make myself as small as I possibly could. They both began to shake as they saw the blood oozing out and Mum started to apologize to him over and over again as he stood there, looking at her, his hand over the wound, the blood seeping through his fingers. Suddenly it was as if they'd never been fighting at all, as if they were a united force.

'I'll drive to the hospital and get it stitched up,' he said matter-of-factly.

He left the house and Mum put on her nightie and began using towels to mop up the trail of blood which led from my room down the stairs, working like a robot.

'Go and wash your face and sort yourself out,' she told me.

When I limped back from the bathroom she sent me down to the kitchen to make her a cup of sweet tea for the shock while she tried to get the stains out of the carpet with soap powder and washing-up liquid. Then she came downstairs, pushing the bloodied towels into the washing machine and rinsing the knife as if removing evidence of her crime. She tidied up my chest of drawers, put all my scattered clothes away neatly and told me to go back to bed once I'd made her tea.

'You're not to say a word to anyone about what's happened,' she warned me, although the whole street must have been able to hear the screams that night. It was to be just one more secret amongst the hundreds that were already cluttering my head and my conscience.

As I climbed back into bed I sent up a prayer that Silly Git would bleed to death on the way to hospital or would become so weak he would crash the car and be killed on impact. I was really excited at the thought of him not coming back. Even if he did try to come back, I reasoned, surely Mum would leave him after all this.

The carving knife wasn't the only weapon that Mum kept handy for when he attacked her. She had other knives around the house and a pair of shears that she kept hidden behind the drainpipe outside the back door. The funny thing was Richard knew all these weapons were there but never did anything about removing them (apart from the brass soldiers), before starting an argument with her. It was as if he enjoyed the danger.

Whenever their fights started, Mum would be screaming at me to call the police and Richard would be shouting at me not to dare. Once or twice I was so frightened he was going to kill her that I ran next door and asked them to phone for help. They did that for me a couple of times, but he made their lives such a misery afterwards that they refused to become involved after that. Eventually, they wouldn't even open the door to me, though no doubt they could hear what was happening through the walls.

Sometimes, when Granddad wasn't living next door, Mum would shout at me to fetch him and I would run up to his house as fast as I could. If I managed to get there in time he would arm himself with a piece of wood and come back with me to break the fight up. Usually, however, Richard would catch me before I got there, carry me back and give me a good hiding for daring to involve other people in a family matter.

In the end everyone had been alienated or intimidated and there was no one left to run to for help, so my brothers and I would sit quietly, not daring to move as Mum and Richard raged around us, just waiting for the fights to exhaust themselves and hoping she wouldn't be killed before his temper had burned itself out.

A few hours after Richard left for the hospital I heard the dreaded sounds of his Cortina returning, his key in the lock and his feet on the stairs. To my horror I realized he was coming into my room first. I lay very still dreading what might come next.

'Janey,' he whispered as I pretended to be asleep, 'I'm really sorry.'

He'd never ever apologized to me for anything before, but maybe he was only doing it now because he believed I was asleep and couldn't hear him. He went back out and closed the door quietly. A few moments later I could hear him and Mum talking in their bedroom.

'I told them the can opener slipped and stabbed me,' he told her.

'You could have come up with something better than that,' she laughed.

They carried on chatting and laughing as if they had just enjoyed a grand adventure together and eventually I fell asleep, disappointed that they had made up and that it didn't sound as if Mum was going to be leaving him.

The next morning they allowed me to lie in, telling the boys to let me sleep. This was another first. I got up and washed when I felt ready and went downstairs, expecting them to be angry with me. When I walked into the front room the sight of my mother shocked me. Her whole face was swollen and bruised and seemed to have changed shape from the beating she'd received. In the drama of the night before I hadn't noticed the damage, or maybe it had taken a few hours to come through. She was barely recognizable.

Richard smiled at me cheerfully, as if this was a normal morning in a normal family. 'Do you want some breakfast?' he asked.

I nodded, not sure how to react to all this. To be allowed to lie in and then to have Richard make me breakfast was unheard of. I kept thinking there must be a catch. All day I was allowed to sit around and not asked to do anything. I wonder now if perhaps I was as bruised as my mother, because Richard had often kept me off school in the past when he had gone too far and left physical marks. I had no way of checking my appearance. The only mirror in the house was in Mum's room, so I only got to look in it if I was vacuuming or taking in some washing.

Although I didn't go back to school for a week that time, Mum and Richard soon got bored with being nice to me and by the next day I was back to doing the household chores. I didn't speak, apart from saying 'yes', 'no', 'please' and 'thank you' for a few days, until Richard had had enough and shouted at me for being a 'sulky cunt' and it was back to business as usual.

~

We all lived in hope that Richard would leave us, and those hopes were fulfilled when he got himself a girlfriend.

The first I heard of it was when Mum refused to iron his shirt for him one day.

'Get your black fucking whore to iron it for you!' she screamed.

He must have been waiting for an excuse, because he left immediately. The boys and I were over the moon and begged Mum not to ask him back.

'We don't want him back, do we, Mum?' we said. 'It's all nice now.'

'Don't you worry,' she assured us. 'He won't be back.'

She must have believed that herself, because a few days later she accepted a friend's invitation to go out to the pub, which was something she would never do without Richard's permission. While she was out he arrived back, bearing a big gold necklace as a peace offering. When he realized she'd gone out and was having a good time, his mood changed immediately. He waited like a thunderstorm brewing on the horizon. I'll never forget the look of terror on her face when she breezed back in and found him there.

I don't know what happened with the other woman; she was never mentioned again.

Thinking back now, with all that I have found out, I begin to wonder how much Mum did know about what was going on. There was one occasion particularly which didn't make sense.

Richard was always very proud of his sheds, which he would build himself at the bottom of every garden he moved to. He built at least three different ones in the years I lived with him. They were very well built, even using proper windows, which we then had to clean as if they were part of the house. Inside, Richard's belongings were always immaculately neat and orderly, like everything else in his life.

Sometimes I would have to go in there with him to 'help him sort out his tools' and he would lock the door behind us. The door had four or five bolts and a chain on the inside, so there was never any chance of us being disturbed. It was only later, when I thought back to those times, that it occurred to me how weird it was that no one else questioned why he was so keen to secure the door from the inside. To me it was just the way things were.

I remember that on this occasion he took me in there while the boys were playing in the garden outside, locked the door and made me stand in front of the window and watch for anybody coming.

'Make yourself look busy,' he instructed, pulling his trousers down to his ankles and standing behind the door. He crouched down and I felt him sliding his hand into my knickers, playing around with me while he masturbated himself. Just a few yards away I could see Mum washing up in the kitchen. Every so often she would look up out of the window and shout at the boys to stay off the grass and on the patio, away from the shed, which was strange, as it was summertime and they were usually allowed to play on the grass at that end of the garden.

I was staring straight into my mother's eyes as I pretended to be tidying up the work surface.

That night I had to hide my knickers inside my dirty clothes because Richard's hands had left big black grease marks and I was frightened Mum would see them and know what was happening.

Richard's mum seemed to hate me almost as much as he did and was always pinching and poking at me when we went round there. She and Mum got on quite well, going to bingo together and everything, but when I was tiny Mum used to make sure she stood between Nan and me.

Nan lived about five miles away from our house to begin with and Richard often used to take me with him on visits because it involved long walks through the woods. We would always have to stop on the way there or back so that I could do him a favour. If there were too many people around and he wasn't able to get me alone he would become really angry and we would have to keep walking until we found a secluded spot. Sometimes he got so carried away with it all we wouldn't have time to go and see his mum and would have to go straight back home after doing it.

On one of these occasions we were meant to be borrowing some sugar or something and when we got back Mum asked for it. When she saw we didn't have it, she asked if we had actually been to Nan's.

'No,' Richard said, obviously worried she might ask Nan.

'Yes,' I said simultaneously, assuming he would want me to lie.

'I mean, no,' I corrected myself quickly, pretending not to see Mum's perplexed expression.

When Nan said she needed a fireplace building in her front room Richard agreed to do it for her, and of course I had to go with him every day. Nan had gone away while the work was being done but one of my cousins was living there and wanted me to play with her when I went round.

One day Richard said I could play out for a bit. 'As long as you don't go too far,' he warned.

After a while he called me back in and I knew what it was for.

'I'll come in with you,' my cousin said.

'No, don't,' I begged her. 'I'll be back in a minute.' But she wouldn't listen. She was getting annoyed with Richard and me because she didn't understand why I always had to be with him.

When he saw her coming in with me he became angry, just as I knew he would. He told her to go back out.

'No,' she replied. 'I live here. I can do what I want.'

My blood would always run cold when other people argued with my stepfather, as I knew that he would be taking his anger out on me later. Now he wasn't going to climb down and became so angry that eventually my cousin went upstairs, shouting abuse as she went.

'Fuck off!' he shouted after her. 'You fat ugly bitch!'

He then took me into the front room, where he was building the fireplace, shut the door and leaned against it, pulling his trousers down and telling me to masturbate him while he played with my chest.

After a few minutes I heard my cousin coming downstairs, calling me to come back outside. She tried to open the door but Richard was leaning his full weight against it, shouting at her to fuck off or he was going to hit her. Eventually she gave up and went outside, shouting as she went. He finished himself off but still wouldn't let me go with her, forcing me to stay in the living room with him and watching while he worked. When Nan got home he told her how bad my cousin had been and how she needed a good hiding, and made me back him up.

His Cortina provided him with another venue for getting me on my own. He would take me with him as he drove around the various DIY stores that he liked, making me sit or lie on the floor in the back with my arm round his seat so that I could masturbate him in the front while he drove. I always knew what he was planning because he would go to the toilet before we left and get a wad of toilet roll or a rag to clear up his mess. Sometimes it would take ages to finish him off as we drove around the lanes and my arm would be burning with pain from the angle I had to work from, but I wouldn't dare to stop until he told me to. If it was dark and we had reached somewhere deserted, we would pull up and he would let me sit in the front seat next to him to do it. When I got older and was too big to squat in the back, I would sit beside him with a newspaper or jumper over my arm while I did it for him.

Once we were at the DIY stores he would make me swap the stickers on the products he wanted with cheaper ones. He was always looking for an angle to get out of paying his way. I used to walk around behind him, terrified that one of the shop assistants would challenge him or not treat him with the respect he felt he deserved and he would start a vicious fight in the aisles.

His car gave him a whole other area to vent his aggressions on the rest of the world. If any other motorist did anything to offend him, like changing lanes in front of him, driving too close or causing him to slow down, he would go after them. If their windows were open he would shout abuse and spit at them. Once he'd caught up with them and forced them to stop he would be out of the car and attacking them with his wheel brace. If it was a woman driver he would send my mother to do his dirty work or, when I was old enough to pick fights with adults, me.

He was always thinking of new night-time rituals for us, particularly if Mum was out of the house, as he knew the boys would never dare to disturb us.

'Stand on the bed,' he ordered me when I was still very tiny. 'Take your clothes off. Turn round.'

When I was standing, naked, with my back towards him he would turn as well, so we were back to back, then put his arms back round me and stretch my body across his back, making my spine crunch painfully. Afterwards I would be paralysed for a few moments, unable to move because of the pain.

As I got older and too heavy to hoist onto his back, he would pour lotion on both of our naked bodies, rub it around and then lie me on top of him, sliding me up and down, rubbing his penis on my vagina. He would then swap so he was on top, but he never penetrated me.

Another game he enjoyed would be making me strip naked in the living room and kneel. I would have to hold my arms out straight and he would place the *Encyclopaedia Britannica* on them. The book had come into the house from a salesman who had called one afternoon while we were all out the front washing the car. Usually anyone who came to the door like that was told to piss off, but for some reason this man caught their attention. Maybe Richard was in a particularly good mood, or maybe the salesman uttered the magic word 'free'. I watched open-mouthed as Richard bantered with him, wondering what angle he was about to work. The man was offering some sort of deal that meant that if they signed up they would receive a couple of free volumes or something. Richard convinced him that he should leave the free volumes anyway and maybe they would sign up later. When the man came back later, of course he was told to piss off. I don't remember anyone in the family ever actually looking inside the books.

Now they were a new means of torture. As my arms began to shake, Richard would add another volume and then he would balance his brown glass Britvic pub ashtray on top. If my arms dropped at all, the ashtray would slide off and he would kick me in the back or the head, shouting at me like a sergeant major to keep my arms up. The agony was intense and when my arms would shake with the strain it would make him even angrier. He seemed to enjoy that sort of torture almost as much as the sexual ones.

When my real life became unbearable I used to retreat inside my head into a fantasy world. Sometimes I would imagine that I was Cinderella, slaving away for my evil stepfather rather than my evil stepmother, and that one day my Fairy Godmother would come and I would be taken to the ball to meet Prince Charming, who would whisk me away from home and marry me. If I could convince myself, even for a few minutes, that there was going to be a happy ending to my story, then I could keep going.

At other times I began to think I was Jesus and I had come back down to Earth to suffer some more in order to save people, just like he did in the Bible. If there was some point to my suffering, then it was easier to bear.

Many years later, when I told these fantasies to a psychologist, he said he thought they might have been what kept me sane through those years, life rafts which allowed me to believe that things would be better one day and that all the suffering wasn't for nothing.

When I was at senior school a girl called Tanya came back to the school after being taken away because of being bullied. I happened to be outside the head of year's study on the morning she arrived. I'd been caught smoking, which happened frequently and which the head of year had given up trying to do anything about, as he knew my parents encouraged me. Tanya was sitting beside me.

'What are you doing here?' I asked.

'I've got to come back,' she said. 'I couldn't get into any other school.'

At that moment a group of the girls who had been bullying her came past, making threatening sucking noises with their teeth, and I could see she was really frightened.

We were both called into the head of year's study together. 'Right, Jane,' he said. 'I'm going to put Tanya in your class and you've got to look after her.' From that moment we became inseparable.

Right away I could see that we were going to have to face down the gang that was bullying Tanya. She was even frightened to go into the toilets because she knew they would follow her in and give her a hard time.

'I'll wait till I get home,' she said.

'No,' I said. 'You go to the toilet when you want to. I'll come in with you.'

Sure enough, they followed us in and started mixing it. I think my experiences with Silly Git had made me especially sensitive to bullying. I just couldn't stand it. There was another girl in the year below us who was a bit of a pitiful figure, always smelling of wee and covered in nits. She used to be bullied so much she would have fits and I started sitting next to her on the bus so that I could protect her, but I would have to get off a few stops before her and the moment the bus pulled away I would see them all jumping on her. I really hated having to leave her with them every day.

Anyway, the gang never bothered Tanya again once I'd made it clear that if they did they would be bothering me as well. I daresay they were wary of me, aware that I came from a family that was known for its violence. The training in aggression that Richard and Mum had given me had actually come in useful for once. I think being well liked by everyone helped too, as no one had any reason to fall out with me.

Tanya and I used to do everything together and she would come to our house to knock for me in the mornings so we could walk to school together. Sometimes Silly Git would give her a hard time when he found her in the house, swinging her round by her ponytail until her feet came off the floor, for instance, which was something he used to do all the time to me, pretending it was all just fun. Another time she arrived proudly wearing a big new clip in her hair and he simply snatched it off her head, dropped it on the floor and stamped on it.

'You don't have to knock for me,' I told her after one of these incidents, 'just wait on the corner till I come out.'

'No,' she said. 'I don't care.'

One evening we were due to go down to a fair together. Tanya came to knock for me at the time I'd told her, but Richard deliberately kept me hanging around for an extra hour and a half doing my chores, so she had to wait. It was a long walk to the fair and I was told I had to be back in early, so we had hardly any time there. Tanya was really fed up about it and asked me why Richard acted so weirdly all the time. We had become so close by then that I decided I could tell her the truth. She was the first person I'd told since Hayley. She was obviously shocked, but didn't get silly about it and I was glad that I had decided to take her into my confidence.

A few days later Mum had gone out unexpectedly and Richard had decided to make me do him a favour in the front room after school. He was just getting into his stride when there was a knock on the front door.

'That fucking cunt Tanya's at the door,' he said after peeking through the curtains. 'I'll get rid of her.'

He went out into the hall and I heard him going to the door and opening it.

'She ain't fucking here,' he snarled.

'Oh, right,' I heard Tanya say, 'so where is she?'

'She's buying a toothbrush over the Parade.'

He slammed the door shut and came back into the front room. 'If you do it good,' he said, 'you can go out and find her afterwards.'

I found Tanya a little while later sitting in the churchyard near the Parade.

'You've just come from there, haven't you?' she said, nodding back towards the house. 'I knew you weren't over the Parade, that's why I've been sitting here. He didn't even have the decency to do his flies up.'

I could just imagine how horrible she must have felt as she sat amongst the graves, knowing that he was doing that to her friend.

Chapter Five

I was quite a late developer, very skinny and undeveloped, and I didn't have my first period until I was fourteen. I remember the moment exactly because I was round at Granddad's, cleaning his stairs, when it came. I rushed home to find Mum and bumped straight into Richard.

'Where are you going?' he demanded.

'I need to talk to Mum,' I said, trying to get past, unable to bring myself to discuss anything so personal with him.

'What do you want to talk to her about?' he wanted to know. I was never allowed to talk to Mum until I'd told him what it was about. I guess he was always wary I might let one of our secrets slip out.

'It's girls' stuff,' I said, hoping he would get the message and back off.

'Oh right,' he said, not only immediately seeming to grasp what I was on about but also seeming to be incredibly concerned. 'Get in there then, young lady,' he said, pushing me towards the living room as he yelled for Mum to come.

They laid me down on the sofa and the boys were sent to get pillows to prop up my head and my legs. 'Go get her some Doctor White's,' Mum said and Richard went scurrying off to the shops. 'You're a lady now,' they kept saying, insisting that I didn't exert myself in any way.

They gave me a few days off school while I continued 'becoming a lady' and I thought it was a pretty good scam. Had I realized how terrible my periods were going to be in the coming months, sometimes lasting for three weeks at a time with one week intervals in between, I might not have been so keen. The pampering wore off pretty quickly too. My periods also worked against me as they gave Mum and Richard more reasons to keep me off school.

I loved going to school because it meant that for a few hours each day I could do and say whatever I wanted and I wouldn't have to pay any gruesome penalties. I revelled in my freedom and was always the class clown, known by pupils and teachers alike for my loud honking laugh and high spirits. The teachers never seemed to mind my behaviour because, unlike many of the children in that school, I was never rude and was always co-operative. I just bubbled over with the joy of escaping the house. Everyone, staff and pupils alike, always seemed to like me, which puzzled me. If I was the despicable creature that my stepdad kept telling me I was, how come no one else could see it?

Knowing that I was liked at school improved my spirits still further when I was there and made dragging myself home at the end of each day even more of an ordeal.

In the beginning I did alright, top of the class sometimes, but as I got older and I was expected to do homework and put in the extra hours, I started to fall behind. I daresay in other schools my lack of academic results would have counted against me, but in an area like ours the teachers were happy just to have someone cheerful and enthusiastic in the classroom. They knew that I was doing my best, but that I had difficulties at home.

I must have been different from most abused children, which is probably why none of the authorities picked up on my problem. Normally they're on the lookout for children who are withdrawn and having difficulty within their peer group, as well as for the obvious signs of bruising and other marks. Many years later Hayley told me that I did always seem to have to wear long sleeves because of bruises on my arms, but I wasn't particularly aware of that. Most of the tortures my stepfather inflicted on me left no visible marks – the scars were all inside my head – and if ever I was badly marked I was kept off school until I had healed.

There was, however, one occasion during my first year in the juniors when my eye had turned completely blood-shot and I was called into the headmaster's office to talk about it. When I got there I found there were some social workers waiting to see me. They must have known something else was going on because the teacher asked, 'Did your father say he was going to kill you?'

I opened my mouth to say 'yes' but at that moment Silly Git burst into the room, sweating as if he had run all the way from the house. I guess they must have been legally bound to let him know or something.

'No,' I said quickly. 'He only says things like that when he's joking, like everyone does.'

'Does he hit you?' they asked me.

'No,' came out of my mouth, although inside my head I was screaming, 'Yes!'

Richard told them all to fuck off, dragged me out of my chair and took me straight home, giving me a good hiding for getting the social workers involved in our family business.

I never heard anything from any of the others. I guess they were happy to take my answers at face value.

Although the authorities probably had no reason to believe that I was being abused in the way I was, they certainly knew that my parents were difficult, violent and abusive. The teachers knew that on Mondays I wouldn't be coming in to school because I would be picking up their social security cheques. All the people in our area who had trouble making their money last would be queuing up at the post office at the same time, the line sometimes reaching round several blocks. Even if you got there at 7.30 in the morning, you might not actually reach the counter until lunchtime, as two people tried to deal with the never-ending tide of people. There was no way Mum and Richard were going to be waiting that long in a queue themselves, so I would be sent instead. I wasn't the only kid in the area being given that responsibility.

Whenever there was a problem at home that meant Mum was out a lot, like the months Les spent in hospital for his burns or when she went into hospital herself to have her kidney out and other operations, or to have another baby, I would be absent from school for weeks on end, shut up in the house doing chores for Silly Git, and I would never be allowed to do any catching up on the work I'd missed.

The teachers knew that I wouldn't be able to do the homework they set me either because my parents believed that my time at home should be dedicated to the family and not to schoolwork. They probably assumed that meant I was sitting around watching television all evening rather than working like a slave scrubbing out the house and looking after the boys. They didn't make a fuss over it – Mum had told them clearly that not only did I not do homework, I didn't do detentions either, and they had enough problems in their working lives without picking fights with her and Richard, so they just encouraged me whenever they had the chance. When I passed a few GCSEs they all went out of their way to tell me how proud they were of me. I was surprised, because I knew I could have done much better if I'd only been allowed to study, and I was grateful to them for their kindness.

Studying of any kind was seen as a sign of snobbishness in our house. If you were found reading a book it was assumed you were putting on airs and graces and trying to prove that you were better than your parents, so none of us did it. When the school said that my brother Pete was exceptionally bright and should be put forward for a scholarship to a nearby private school, Richard said no. His excuse was he didn't want his son going to 'a school for gay boys', but I guess he felt it would lessen his control over Pete and take him into an environment where he would be out of his depth.

I don't know whether the school staff made any effort to persuade the authorities to intervene on my behalf with my family, and since my files have gone missing I am never likely to find out, but I do know there was nothing they could have done themselves without running the risk of being intimidated and even attacked in their own classrooms or on the way in or out of school. Their hearts must have sunk every time they saw another child arrive at the school with our surname, knowing it would mean being abused and shouted at during parents' evenings. In the end they managed to get Richard banned from the junior school for his aggressive behaviour, although I can't imagine how they enforced the ban.

If I had only known that the kindly dinner lady who always asked me how I was as I queued up for my meals was actually asking on behalf of my dad, I might have been able to get a message back to him, telling him that things were going badly and asking him to come and get me. As it was, I just thought she was a nice lady and that my dad had disowned me. The dinner lady would have seen a loud cheerful girl, eating hearty meals despite her skinny frame. There would have been no reason for her to tell Dad anything other than that I looked fine and that he didn't need to worry.

Richard must have liked the look of me in a school uniform. I assume that was why he made me wear the stupid high-heeled court shoes when I was in junior school, and he made his tastes even more obvious as I grew older. When I was a teenager and Mum was out of the house, he would have me put on my PE skirt, long socks and top, put my hair up and slap on some make-up. He would then lie on the bed and masturbate as I walked around the room, bending over and opening drawers so he could see my knickers. I would then have to climb onto the bed and finish him off.

Chapter Six

Mum and Silly Git basically saw education as an imposition that their children needed to shake off as quickly as possible, and even before it was legal for me to leave school they told me I needed to go out and earn a living in order to pay my way around the house.

It started out with work experience organized by the school and when the teachers asked me what I wanted to do, I said I would like to do something with small children. Although it had been too much at times, I'd enjoyed looking after my brothers when they were little, particularly Les, who had been more my baby than Mum's really. Whenever I was at home he was always with me. Even if I went out to be with a friend or up to my room, I always had to take him with me. It wasn't his fault – Mum and Richard just didn't want the bother of having to look after him themselves – but it annoyed my friends to always have him tagging along.

Les ended up spoilt, though, because even though they didn't want to look after him, Mum and Richard let him have his own way all the time. If he wanted to have something of mine I had to let him, otherwise he would scream and they would intervene on his behalf and I would lose whatever it was forever. He was even allowed to call Mum a 'fat slag' and Silly Git would just laugh and encourage him.

When Les was a baby and I was eleven, it was my job to get up to him if he cried in the night and I had to take him into bed with me to keep him quiet. I was so frightened of doing it wrong that on the nights when he slept through I would wake up in a dazed state and think I'd lost him because he wasn't in the bed with me. I would be crawling around the floor on my hands and knees in the dark trying to find him before I woke up enough to remember he wasn't there.

One afternoon Mum and I went round to visit my granddad and I was starting to tell him about how I'd been crawling around the floor in the middle of the night looking for Les.

'Shut up!' Mum hissed and I realized I'd spoken out of turn.

'Why was she doing that then?' Granddad asked, obviously puzzled.

'Oh you know her,' Mum brushed it aside, 'she's just a fucking div, isn't she?'

I realized that she wouldn't want her dad to know that she was making me do her job of caring for the baby. I learnt to keep quiet after that.

As he got older Les became so spoilt he was impossible to deal with, so it was Tom and Dan, the middle two, who ended up being my favourite brothers.

Silly Git didn't like the idea of me working with children, though, because it wouldn't be of any use to him. He wanted me working in the high street. If I was stacking shelves in one of the supermarkets, he reasoned, I would be getting discounts on food for the family. In the end he and Mum found me a job in a shoe shop, insisting that I hand over whatever money I earned for my board and lodging and only leaving me enough for my bus tickets to and from work and sandwiches for lunch. It was like living with playground bullies who nick the pocket money off little kids.

Although I would like to have stayed on at school for longer and got a few more qualifications, I actually enjoyed the job and didn't mind doing it full time. Just like school, it meant I was out of the house and safely away from Richard for a few hours every day, although he was always waiting for me when I got home.

I was amazed by how well I got on with everyone in the shop. No one was ever nasty to me, quite the opposite. Although the manageress was sometimes quite strict with the other girls, she seemed to like me, taking me outside with her every time she wanted a cigarette break and leaving the others holding the fort. 'Me and Jane are just going out for a fag,' she would announce to the others, and we would sweep majestically away. None of the others seemed to hold it against me, though.

The manageress's husband also took to me and used to ask me to go out shopping with him whenever he had to buy things for his wife and needed some female advice. There was even talk of me being given a branch of my own with a flat above it, although nothing came of it.

The fact that everyone except my own family seemed to like me was probably what kept me from completely giving up on life in those early years. Although Richard managed to frighten me into obeying his every command, he never managed to convince me that I was quite the vile worm that he told me I was. If I could just find a way to escape his clutches, I knew there was a nice world out there full of nice people I could have a laugh with. It was just that I couldn't work out how to get away from him in order to reach it.

Despite all the things that he did to me physically, Richard still seemed to have a fantasy life about me as well. When I was about sixteen I came home one evening from work while it was still light. Mum had taken the boys to their boxing lesson, as she always did now, and when I walked in Richard told me to have a bath immediately so the water would be hot again for the others later.

I went upstairs with a heavy heart, assuming he was going to be using it as an excuse to come into the bathroom and abuse me. There was nothing I could do to keep him out because he'd taken the lock off the door, saying that he didn't want any locked doors in his house, which was a bit ironic given the state of his shed and all the outside doors. I guess an internal locked door would have limited his power to go wherever he wanted in the house whenever he wanted. If any one of the inside doors had had a lock we would have been able to escape him, if only for a few minutes at a time, and he wouldn't have been able to tolerate that.

As I undressed I had a strange feeling that something creepy was about to happen. I got into the bath quickly, trying to cover myself, feeling that I was being watched. I couldn't work out if there was a hole in the door where the lock had been or not. I rushed my bath, climbed out and swung the door open quickly, wondering if it was all in my mind, and wasn't able to stop myself from screaming as I almost tripped over Richard kneeling on the floor with his jeans and pants around his ankles and his penis in his hand. I slammed the door shut and heard him scuffling around outside, gathering himself together. When I was sure he'd gone to his bedroom I dried myself as fast as I could and went to my bedroom to dress. The incident was never mentioned again, which was odd since Richard was never usually embarrassed when it came to talking about his urges and what he was going to be doing to me.

Usually he would try to make out that everything he did was a joke. Sometimes when I was in the kitchen washing up he would creep up behind me and stick a plastic carrier bag over my head or wrap my face in cling film. He would be laughing and I wouldn't be able to fight back or say it was hurting or frightening me because then I would be in trouble for being 'moody'. The first few times I instinctively fought to get the bags off, just as I had tried to fight my way out from underneath the pillows he put over my face, or I would try to push a hole through the plastic to my mouth so that I could get some air, but it only made him angry so I changed my tactics, as I had with the pillows, and just stood there, trying to carry on with the washing up as if nothing was happening, fighting to overcome the urge to panic. I hoped it would make the game too boring for him, but it just angered him because he thought I wasn't playing along in the right spirit. I don't know what reaction I could have come up with that would have pleased him. I doubt there was one actually.

His mum had moved away from the area by then and lived a seven-hour drive away. Every so often he used to announce out of the blue that he was taking me to stay with her for a few days. I had to go to help him 'because of his bad leg'. I dreaded the thought of being more or less alone with him for several days in a row, knowing that my nan and granddad would never suspect a thing and wouldn't be able to do anything to protect me even if they'd wanted to.

The reason Nan had moved was in order to live next to her sister in one of those bungalows for old people, which meant she was next door drinking tea most of the time we were there. Granddad was past noticing anything, having reached the stage of putting his shoes in the fridge and making himself teabag sandwiches. He was a nice old boy who had worked all his life as a cabinet-maker, never taking a day off and always beavering away in his shed. I never heard him swear once, which made him very different from the rest of the family. The day he retired he started to go a bit funny in the head. I guess his work had provided an escape from the reality of his marriage.

Their bungalow was in a little hamlet of about ten houses and one shop. I remember the house opposite kept a huge seal in a pond in their garden. They'd rescued it after it was washed ashore in a storm as a baby and had looked after it ever since. It snowed one year when my stepdad and I were up there and I was trapped in the house with him for a week, with him acting like we were a couple or something.

Although Nan was never nice to me when I was a child, she did relent when I was about sixteen. She had just been told she had cancer and she called me over to her chair to tell me that she was sorry for everything and that she did love me really. It made me cry my eyes out, especially as she died not long after that.

Richard had a sister, too, who was as aggressive as he was. I remember Mum telling me she walked into a pub with her once and my aunt plonked one of her feet on the bar and asked a complete stranger if he liked her 'fucking boots'. She was one of the few people who would fight Richard back, hitting as hard as he did. Once she went for him with her stiletto heel.

The night before we were due to leave on one of our trips to Nan's, Richard and I were in the kitchen at home together. Mum had gone next door with Les to borrow the phone and the other boys were in the front room watching television. Richard started telling me all the things he and I would be doing on the way there and back, as well as while we were there. It was as if he thought I would be as pleased and excited as he was at the prospect. I was becoming angrier and angrier and I kept hearing a song in my head that had been featured on the television series *Grange Hill*, 'Just say no'. I'd been thinking about those lyrics for years and for some reason, when Richard asked me if I wanted to do all those things, I just said, 'No.'

I immediately knew I'd made a huge mistake. He pressed his forehead against mine, his eyes drilling into my eyes, cold and angry, his breath on my face.

'What?'

I don't know why, but I said 'No' again. It was as if some tiny spark of courage had finally been kindled into a flame deep inside my head.

His fist came up from nowhere and punched my head back against the tiles of the wall behind me. I started crying and tried to say sorry, but I'd made him too angry to be able to calm down now. Lost in a black fog of anger, he punched me over and over again, then grabbed my hair, dragging me away from the wall and literally kicking me into the air and out into the hallway, past the open door to the front room where my brothers were sitting. When I landed he chased after me, still kicking and shouting and telling me I was 'an ungrateful cunt'. My brothers were screaming from the sofa for him to stop, frightened he was going to kill me, but none of them daring to move, knowing that he would turn his fury on them if they tried to interfere.

We all heard Mum's key in the door.

'Get up and sort yourself out,' Richard ordered.

I stood up and tried to tidy myself as he yelled at the boys to shut up. There were clumps of my hair on the pristine red carpet and my face was blotchy from the blows. As Mum walked in I straightened myself up. The boys were silent, white-faced and shaky.

Mum must have been able to hear the screams from next door and from outside, but she was as anxious as the boys not to have Richard turn on her next.

'What's wrong with you?' she asked me, sounding mildly irritated to find that I was making a fuss about something yet again.

'Something in my eye,' I replied, a line I often used to explain why it might look as if my eyes were watering.

As always, Mum accepted what I said at face value and didn't ask anything else.

Considering how controlling Richard was about everything I did and everywhere I went, he was surprisingly keen for me to get a boyfriend and start having sex, and he put me on the pill as soon as he could, even before I had left school. The fact that my periods were so incessant and painful gave him an ideal excuse.

He also suggested that a girlfriend and I went down to Southend with a couple of boys to stay in my uncle's caravan. In the end the boys weren't able to get away from work, but my friend and I still went and met up with some other boys when we were down there. It was a brilliant holiday, except for one incident when one of the boys was messing about with a big pebble which my cousins must have brought in from the beach and varnished. He was chucking it from hand to hand while standing in front of the caravan window and catching it just in time. I was asking him not to and then he missed the catch and it hit the window. I went mental, imagining how much trouble I was going to get into for this, and I made the poor boy call out someone at Bank Holiday rates to replace the window.

It was a great holiday, but it left me puzzled as to why I had suddenly been allowed to do something so grown up. It gave me a shred of hope that maybe things were going to get better.

When I got back home one of the boys we had met sent me a love letter. Richard intercepted my post as always and read it out loud to the whole family while I sat there crying my eyes out, feeling humiliated and realizing I wasn't free yet.

There was a boy called Nick living in our street who was a year older than me and had already left school to become a scaffolder, and I thought he was fantastic. All the girls fancied him. Hayley and I used to watch him walking past our houses from behind net curtains, giggling and sighing and fantasizing about him asking us out. I would never have let him know how I felt because I would have been too embarrassed and because I wouldn't have wanted my stepdad to know that I fancied someone in case he turned nasty on them.

I was coming back from school as normal one afternoon and as I approached the house I knew the sitting room had been stripped out in order to be redecorated yet again. The giveaway sign was that the windows had been smeared with Windolene so that people couldn't see in while the curtains were down. As I went in Richard greeted me in a particularly good mood. Decorating always seemed to make him happy.

The windows were open to let out the fumes from the paint and from inside the room I saw Nick coming down the street, going towards his house. Richard spotted him as well and must have seen something in my expression because he started singing, 'Love is in the air! Janey's in love with Nick.'

I could see that Nick could hear and just wanted to curl up and die. Then Richard started calling out to him like a stupid schoolkid: 'Janey loves you, Nick!'

He wrote the same message in the Windolene with his finger for everyone, including Nick, to see. I had to laugh with him or I would have been in trouble for being a miserable cow, but actually I was just shrivelling up from embarrassment.

Richard wasn't going to let it drop either. Every day Nick would walk past the house and Richard would shout at him again, until eventually he got a grinning response out of the boy and finally he was inviting him in for a cup of tea. Nick's visits began to become a regular thing and I started to go out with him. Although I'd been so angry with Richard at the beginning, I had to admit that this was a bit of a result for me, as I'd fancied Nick for so long and would never have plucked up the courage to talk to him myself.

I began to think that maybe this would mark the end of the abuse. If Richard was matching me up with someone else, maybe he was planning to leave me alone himself. Perhaps now that I was no longer a child, he was finally losing interest in me and would be willing to let me step out from under his tyrannical rule.

I don't know why I was so optimistic. There had already been so many times when I'd thought that maybe Richard would change his ways. I'd hoped he would stop when I reached puberty and with every birthday since I'd hoped that he would lose interest in me, but it never happened. Occasionally I would ask if we could stop doing things and he would say we could, as long as I did him 'one last special favour'. I would do whatever it was, but it wouldn't make any difference, he'd find an excuse for me to do something else again the next day.

Sometimes I would try to use my period as an excuse for why we couldn't do something he wanted, occasionally lying about the dates, but he even found a way of turning that against me.

'You dirty little bitch,' he shouted at me as he came downstairs from the bathroom one day. 'You left your fucking jam rags in the toilet and I had to flush them away.'

I knew he'd made it up because I wasn't on my period, even though I'd told him I was, and I knew for a fact it was nothing to do with Mum, but I couldn't say anything or I would have given myself away. I think he just got a kick out of talking to me in a degrading way. But if I actually had a boyfriend, I told myself, things were bound to be different. He wasn't going to want to share me, was he?

As soon as I realized Richard was going to allow it, I spent as much time as I could at Nick's house. His family were so nice. His mum really seemed to approve of me for her boy. She would buy me gold jewellery and even had a picture of Nick and I together up on her wall.

'I always hoped you would go out with my Nick,' she told me over and over again, making me feel really special and wanted.

One day Nick took me up to London for a trip on one of the tour buses. I fell completely in love and believed that I had finally found a way out of my terrible life.

Although Silly Git was encouraging us to be together all the time, he was also warning Nick off doing anything he would regret in the half-jokey sort of voice that he used most of the time. 'You mess with her,' he'd warn, 'and I'll be cutting your fucking dick off!' As usual it was impossible to tell from his tone whether he was joking or serious.

It was confusing, but I was so happy. For the first time in my life I felt truly loved and part of a kind family. I knew that Nick would never ever do anything to hurt me and he never pressured me about sex.

The only bad part was that Silly Git demanded that I do him a lot more favours in exchange for all the times he let me go round to Nick's house, making me feel dirty before I even started. He would tell Mum he was paying me to cut the lawn or clean the car, but then tell me that it was really to do him a favour. It was beginning to dawn on me that he was actually paying me to do him favours in exchange for my freedom. He had turned me into something close to a prostitute as well as a slave, and I hated him for it. But at least while I had Nick there was hope that I would eventually be free, that I would soon be leaving home and spending my life with a man who loved me and was kind to me. I was falling in love for the first time and it felt very good.

I should have known better. It wasn't long before Silly Git changed the rules of the game again and started to become jealous of the amount of time I spent at Nick's. He would make up reasons why I couldn't go round and then he would make up other reasons why Nick couldn't come round to our house.

'That boy's taking you for a fucking idiot,' he told me one day. 'You have to dump him. Go and do it now and come straight back.'

I could tell from his tone of voice that he'd made up his mind. And once he'd made up his mind, that was it. I had to end the best relationship that had ever happened to me there and then, and I wouldn't be able to explain why because then Nick would want to go round and talk to Richard about it, which would make him furious and I would get a beating. Since Nick had left school and our paths never crossed during the day, I would never even have a chance to get him on his own in order to give him a proper explanation.

I was gutted, but I knew that I wouldn't be able to fight it. Richard had just been teasing me with a glimpse of what a life of freedom might be like and now he was going to snatch it away from me again, just to show that he could.

'Go on, go round and fucking tell him,' he snapped.

I knew that Nick was as besotted with me as I was with him. As well as the stuff from his mum, he had given me some gold necklaces, one of which had a locket containing a picture of us together which I treasured more than anything. Richard told me to give them all back.

'Give him a hard time,' he told me as I went out the door. 'Make him suffer for the way he's treated you.'

I couldn't do that, but I couldn't make it easy for him either, because it would all have to be done quickly so I could get back home before Richard followed me to see why I was taking so long.

I dragged my feet round to Nick's house, feeling that my whole world was about to end. I knew there was nothing I could say which would explain why I was calling a halt to a relationship that had been going so well.

Nick could see something was wrong the moment I came in, but he had no idea I was about to dump him. I wanted to scream and cry and tell him how much I loved him, but instead I had to tell him it was over. I had to keep myself from crying as well, otherwise my eyes would be puffy when I got back home and I would be punished for being miserable. Nick must have thought I was a right hard cow to be able to drop him and not shed a single tear. But if I had told him that Richard had ordered it he would have wanted to go round and sort it out, which would inevitably have led to violence. There was no way Nick would have been able to make Richard change his mind; he was just a teenager.

When I'd explained that it was over and returned the presents I walked back home, knowing that I'd just been made to destroy my chance of experiencing love and happiness. I couldn't even cry when I got back home because I would have received a beating if Richard had caught me. I just had to sit with him, my mind a miserable blur, agreeing with all his stupid reasons for why it had been the right thing to do. The hope of escape that I had been nurturing had been snuffed out and I was back where I started.

When I turned sixteen and was working full time in the shoe shop I hoped once more that things would change and I would be given a bit more freedom. I was occasionally allowed to do the odd thing like going out with friends in the evening, but compared to everyone else of my age, I was still virtually a prisoner.

One night I was allowed to go to a twelve-hour MTV party being held at the local youth club to raise money. There I met a boy called Joe who seemed to be very chilled out, probably because of all the joints he was smoking. He was a bit wayward and not the most ideal boyfriend material, but I liked him because he wasn't loud and mouthy and he didn't seem to be just after sex like the other boys who were asking me out at that stage. They were the sort of blokes who think it's funny to shout, 'Get yer tits out!' at girls as they pass in the street, and I had enough of that sort of thing at home. I was terrified of the thought of having to have sex with anyone after everything I'd experienced, and it was nice to be with someone who didn't put any pressure on me, just as it had been with Nick.

It was three months before Joe and I slept together and when we did it was a nice experience – well, as nice as the first time can be for any girl. By that time I was besotted with him and his gentle ways. I think I would have clung to anyone who was kind to me at that stage.

Despite Joe's unsuitability as a boyfriend, Richard went back into his liberal mode, letting me go out most nights and even allowing me to stay round at Joe's house when I wanted to. It seemed that the rules had changed again, but I was aware they could change back at any moment.

Once Richard invited Joe to come with him and me to visit my nan at her bungalow. I liked the idea of Joe coming with us because I thought that would mean Richard wouldn't be able to get to me, although I was nervous about what sort of humiliation he might have planned for us. He told me that Joe and I would have a separate room, but when we got there I discovered we were all going to be sleeping in the sitting room, Richard on the sofa and Joe and me on the floor. I made sure Joe was next to the sofa.

'I ain't sleeping next to him,' Richard joked. 'You swap over.'

Not being able to tell Joe why I didn't want to swap, I had to do as he said. Once Joe was asleep, Richard's hand crept under the covers and started fiddling with me. I just wanted to die of shame.

Despite all his apparent friendliness, Richard took great pleasure in humiliating Joe in the most childish ways possible, like putting laxatives in his drink or sending him over to the shop and then making me get into the Cortina and drive off with him before Joe got back, leaving him alone for hours while Richard made me masturbate him in the car somewhere. When we eventually got back I had to lie about where we'd been. Joe put up with all of it with really good humour and patience, but then I guess his home life wasn't that great either, and being so young, he wasn't in a position to make a fuss. He was an easygoing chap anyway and Richard wasn't someone you would argue with if you didn't have to.

Joe had said he liked the idea of getting a tattoo. 'Time for you to get this tattoo, young man,' Silly Git said one day and took us both down to the coast for a day out. While we were in the tattoo parlour he made me pay for him to have some swallows put on his hands. He already had Mum's name written on his neck. It was considered quite normal in our family. Mum had quite a few tattoos on her arms. Joe chose to have an eagle on his back.

Now Richard kept asking me if Joe and I had had sex. He made it sound as if he was teasing me, but I suspected a trap so admitted nothing. And anyway, I didn't want to talk about personal things like that with him. I didn't want him to think that I might have done something like that and actually enjoyed it.

In the end, however, he got me down on the kitchen floor with his hand around my throat, slapping me round the face while somehow managing to convince my mum that it was all just a bit of a laugh, and I couldn't hold out any more. Part of me was still grasping at straws, hoping that he would stop making demands on me himself if he thought I was having sex with someone, while another part of me just didn't have the energy to lie about it any more.

'Yes, alright,' I admitted, 'we've had sex.'

I couldn't tell what effect my confession was having. Was I going to get a beating for being a slag? Would he be jealous or would he just make a joke of it? Would it mean that he would finally leave me alone? Would he use it as an excuse to beat up Joe?

I braced myself for a blow, but it never came. My confession didn't send him into one of his rages after all, but it did have a dramatic effect on his attitude to me.

In all the years that my stepfather had been abusing me, he had always been careful not to actually penetrate me. I didn't question this, or wonder why it might be, it was just the way it was and I was grateful for it. It had never occurred to me that if I had told anyone about what he did it would have been very hard for them to prove anything, but if he had been inside me while I was still a virgin, then it would have been much easier. I suppose I assumed that he got his kicks from all the other stuff and that he was happy to save the penetration for Mum. I'd walked in on them in the bedroom once by mistake. She had her back to him and looked to me as if she was asleep, or at least pretending to be, as he humped away. It had made me feel sick. Every Sunday afternoon when I was younger they would go upstairs together, leaving me to look after my brothers until they came down. Sometimes they would be up there for hours, but it would be impossible to keep four boys quiet for that long and Richard would eventually come storming downstairs to punish me for failing in my task.

Now, as soon as he knew that I had had penetrative sex with Joe, he told me that the next time he got me on my own he and I would be doing it as well. 'Now you've already done it,' he said, 'it won't be any different from doing it with him.'

I just nodded, a terrible sense of dread running through me like ice, unable to believe that just when I had hoped it was going to get better, it was actually going to get far, far worse. Despite everything he had done to me over the years, this seemed something much more intimate and vile, even worse than the kissing with tongues. I had always been able to scrub the smell of him off my skin after he'd touched me, but this would be impossible to erase. From now on I was going to be raped regularly and there was nothing I could do to stop it unless I was willing to be beaten to a pulp and watch Mum suffering the same fate.

Also, once he'd discovered that I had lost my virginity, Richard instructed me to dump Joe, just like I'd dumped Nick. I felt my heart breaking all over again as I thought about telling poor sweet Joe that we were over. He used to come and meet me from work and I was going to have to tell him on the bus between work and home, with everyone else listening in. The bus was always packed, but I couldn't risk missing it and being late home. I told him I was going to have to end it and we sat with our heads together, crying for the whole forty-minute ride. People were looking at us as if we were mad. When I got home I told my stepdad that it was done and I managed not to cry in front of him, but I cried whenever I was on my own for months after that.

Suddenly impatient to get what he wanted, Richard started laying his plans for this new stage in our relationship and told Mum that he and I were going out to get some parts for the car. As we walked out of the house together it felt as if someone had filled my stomach with ice cubes. In all the years that he had been torturing and abusing me I had always hung on to the fact that I was lucky he had never actually done this to me, and now he was going to.

'If you do this properly,' he told me as we got into the car, 'you can go out this evening.'

He also told me that this was the last thing I would ever have to do for him, but I knew that was a lie because he had told me that so many times before and there was always a reason why I had to do just one more thing. As a child I might have believed him, but it was no longer possible to fool myself so completely. If he was able to do it to me today, why wouldn't he want to do it again tomorrow, and the next day, and every day after that?

Still, as he was being so nice, and was obviously so keen for me to co-operate, I felt I was a tiny bit in control of the situation, more than I had ever been in the past. I thought it was possible I might be able to get at least one little concession.

'Will you use a condom, please?' I asked, thinking that I couldn't bear the thought of him being inside me and leaving his mess behind him.

'You don't need to use those,' he said, 'you're on the pill.'

'Oh please,' I begged. 'The pill isn't always 100 per cent safe.'

'Okay,' he agreed, and we stopped at a garage to buy some. I felt as if I was on my way to my own execution.

It was the middle of the afternoon. We drove around the country lanes looking for a spot that Richard thought would be safe. Eventually he found a relatively secluded car park. There were a couple of other cars already parked there, one with some people in.

'We'll wait for them to go,' he told me, making me kiss him and touch him while we waited. To any casual passer-by we would have looked like any couple out on a date – a sixteen-year-old girl with a thirty-year-old man, not such an unusual sight – and I hated the fact that anyone might think I was actually with him by choice.

About ten minutes later the people in the other car still weren't showing any signs of going and now and then other people were walking past with their dogs, enjoying the scenery. I was beginning to hope that I would get away with it, for one day at least.

But now that Richard was aroused there was little chance that he was going home without having what he had been thinking about all day. Eventually he couldn't wait a moment longer. He was going to do it whether there was anyone watching or not.

'Lie your chair back,' he instructed. 'Pull your skirt up and take off your knickers.'

He climbed over to my side of the car. Pulling his trousers and pants down, he put on the condom and had full sex with me for the first time. Even after all the years of abuse and humiliation, this still seemed much worse. I couldn't stop myself from crying, even when he ordered me to shut up. The smell of his breath on my face made me feel sick and the fact that he kept kissing me as he was doing it made me want to throw up. I wasn't sure if it was technically a rape, since I'd known he was going to do it and hadn't tried to stop him, but I felt as if I'd been raped. It was almost as if he had spent the previous twelve years preparing me for this.

That year Mum got a job helping out as a secretary at the boxing club my brothers went to. That meant it was just Richard and me in the house three nights a week. When I got home from work at seven the lights would all be out, so I couldn't see where he was, but he would always be there, waiting in the dark, calling me into the living room for sex. I tried to put him off me by not washing properly, but it never made any difference to him. If I was even one minute late home he would throw my dinner in the bin and I would have to go to bed hungry, but I would still have to perform whatever tricks he had been dreaming up for me all day. It seemed the older I got, the more he was going to treat me as his sex slave. I couldn't imagine how I was ever going to escape him now.

Chapter Seven

After Joe came Paul. I met him at a party when I was about to turn seventeen and he walked me home, but I wouldn't let him kiss me goodnight, even though I was very keen to see him again. He must have been keen as well, because he didn't allow my initial reluctance to put him off. He was four years older than me and, as with Joe, I started sleeping with him after we had been going out for about three months.

Richard, no doubt relishing the opportunity for another game of cat and mouse, encouraged the match, even allowing Paul to stay in my room when he was round at our house. Paul was one of those easygoing types that Richard particularly liked because he could make them do pretty much whatever he wanted.

As always, though, it was impossible to know where we were with Richard. One day he would be welcoming Paul into the house and treating him like a friend, the next he would be telling me to get rid of him and becoming angry that he was even daring to knock on the door. I would get into trouble with Richard if Paul came knocking when he didn't feel like seeing him, and I'd also get into trouble with Paul, who never knew whether I was going to invite him in with open arms or send him packing with no explanation. The fact that Richard let us sleep together quite openly, however, seemed like a move forward. I was beginning to be awarded some of the privileges of being an adult.

One morning Paul and I were still asleep in my bed when Silly Git came crashing into the room. He seemed to be looking for something as we struggled to wake up and work out what was going on.

'Where are they?' he wanted to know.

'Where are what?' I asked sleepily.

'Where are your fucking pills?'

'What pills?'

'You know, *the* pill.'

'Over there,' I nodded towards my dressing table. 'Why?'

'Because they're going down the fucking toilet,' he said, taking them out of the drawer and walking out to the bathroom. 'It's time you made me a granddad.'

We could hear him going into the bathroom and then there was the sound of the toilet flushing. My mind was racing, trying to work out what this might mean and whether it was a trick or a potential way out for us. Richard never did anything without a reason and if he wanted us to have a baby it wasn't because he thought it would make us happy. He would be doing it for himself in some way, but I couldn't work out what his angle was. For a while I pretended that I didn't want to have a baby, knowing that if Richard thought he was pleasing me he might change his tack, but secretly I was very happy about the idea of having a baby with Paul, and he didn't seem worried by the prospect either. I really loved him and had been dreaming for some time of starting a family with him. When I'd had time to think it through, I also decided that if I had a child it would be a way to get out of the house and get a place of my own. Finally, I thought, Richard had presented me with a way to escape him.

As always, I grabbed the chance to feel optimistic. If I did become pregnant, perhaps Richard would leave me alone at last. Surely even he wouldn't want to do things to a woman who was pregnant by another man. I hoped this might finally be the end of it all, that he had finally grown tired of me and was willing to let me go and lead a life of my own.

Paul was just as keen on the idea if it meant that we would get a place of our own and be away from Richard's tyrannical whims. Although he knew nothing about what Richard was getting up to with me in secret, he knew that he was an unpleasant, unpredictable and manipulative man to have in your life; he just put up with it in order to be with me and did his best to keep his head down.

For the next three months Paul and I kept trying for a baby, while Richard was careful to use a condom whenever he had sex with me. Each month I was disappointed and then in the third month my period was late. I did a test and it came up positive. I was so happy and so excited at the thought of having a baby of my own. Mum and Richard seemed to be as excited as I was, which was a bit of a puzzle, but I decided to make the most of their approval while it lasted. Maybe once I was a mother everything would change and they would start treating me as an equal.

Just because I'd succeeded in doing what he apparently wanted me to do, however, didn't mean that I was let off my other duties to Richard. 'Now you're pregnant, we don't need to use condoms any more,' he informed me as soon as we were alone. My heart sank. How could I actually have believed that things were going to get better? He had managed to find a way of making them even worse.

In my confused state I became convinced that if I had sex with Richard while I was pregnant the baby might come out half his and half Paul's. I think I knew that couldn't happen, but that was what it felt like. I begged him to go on using condoms or to withdraw, but he wasn't going to listen to anything I had to say. I felt that I was being subjected to the final humiliation. Just when I should have been at my happiest he had managed to make me feel the most suicidal I had ever felt.

I had always harboured ideas of killing myself, even as a child. Almost every day when I walked home from school with Hayley I used to pause on a bridge that went over the park, a place where all the junkies used to hang out, and talk about the attractions of jumping off rather than going home for one more night of hell. Now the idea of oblivion, with no more pain, heartache and humiliation, was becoming even more attractive.

All through the pregnancy, as I grew bigger and more ungainly, I kept believing that Richard would soon stop wanting sex, but it never happened. When my bump became too big for him to lie on top of me he would make me sit in an armchair with my bottom at the front of the cushions and he would kneel on the floor in front of me in order to get what he wanted.

Richard bullied Paul into moving into the house full time, even though he hated Richard as much as anyone else, and then set about making money out of him, charging him rent and then extra for his share of the food, gas and electric. Although he had been living at home with his mum, Paul was used to his freedom and to being treated like an adult. When Mum and Richard told him he could only bath once a day, he couldn't believe it.

'I have two showers a day,' he told them, 'one in the morning and one when I get back from work.'

'You'll have to pay if you want us to put the immersion on just for you,' Richard informed him.

I was deeply grateful to Paul for loving me enough to put up with so much so that we could be together. He was a really good man and I could quite understand why he allowed Richard to bully him. He knew that if he didn't do whatever Silly Git wanted I would be made to split up from him and he didn't want that. We both convinced ourselves that once we had the baby we would be able to escape to a place of our own and our ordeal would be over. We were nearly at the end of it. If we could just last out for a few more months, then there was a chance that life could get better.

Every Sunday Paul would go off to play football and I would have to stay at home to do the ironing for eight people and whatever else Silly Git could dream up for me, when all I wanted to do was go and watch him, like any normal girlfriend. I would beg him not to go, but I couldn't explain to him the true reason so he didn't take my pleas seriously. 'Don't worry,' he would say when I seemed despondent, 'we'll soon be out of here and then you'll be able to do whatever you want whenever you want.' But then he thought it was just housework that was getting me down and I could never tell him the terrible truth.

When I was nine months pregnant and exhausted, both by the pregnancy and by the emotional strains of the family, I was alone in the house with Richard one afternoon and he became cross with me for 'looking miserable' while I swept the stairs with a hand brush. He ordered me to scrub the kitchen floor with my toothbrush as a penance for being a 'sulky cow'. Frightened of angering him any further, in case he hit me and damaged the baby, I sank miserably to my knees and starting scrubbing.

Mum came home in the middle of it all. 'What are you doing?' she asked.

'Scrubbing the floor,' I said wearily.

'What are you using?' She was looking at me as if I was mad.

'My toothbrush.'

'Why?'

'He told me to,' I said as Richard came into the room behind her.

He immediately pretended to be amazed to find that I was actually doing it, insisting that he had been joking but that I was too much of a 'silly bitch' to realize it.

At that moment something inside my head snapped and I knew I couldn't take it any more. I didn't know what new games he was planning for me and my baby, but I couldn't cope with them. I just wanted to end it for both of us. I didn't want my baby to have to come into this awful life.

I went up to my bedroom and looked around for something that I could use to cut my wrists. I found a Bic razor and tried to snap the blade away from the handle.

Mum came in and stopped me. 'Don't be such a stupid little fucking bitch,' she told me.

'But he just never stops,' I sobbed.

'If you kill yourself then you've given him what he fucking wants,' she said.

I could see she was right, but I felt so tired of it all I wasn't sure if I cared any more. Still I gave up on my feeble suicide attempt and went back to struggling on, hoping for the best.

When Emma was born she was beautiful and I was so proud of her. Knowing that I now had a baby who was dependent on me to protect her made me doubly determined to get out of the house, just as soon as I could arrange alternative accommodation with the council. Surely now it would only be a matter of a few weeks before we were free.

Richard and Mum came into the hospital to visit me and bought flowers and a card. It sounds such a normal thing for parents to do when their daughter has a baby, but they had never done anything like that for me before in my life, or for anyone else for that matter. It was the most alien thing imaginable. On one hand it made me think that perhaps we really had turned a corner and now that I was a mother everything would be different, but on the other hand it made me wonder what Richard was up to now. It seemed that he was genuinely thrilled by the arrival of his first grandchild, especially as she was a girl, but how many times had he lulled me into a false sense of security before, only to dash my hopes with some new horror?

Mum and Richard might have been sweet to me, but something had gone very wrong between them and two days later, when I was on the verge of being discharged, Mum turned up at the hospital with her face beaten to a pulp, black and swollen, and her ear caked in dry blood.

'He just went fucking loopy,' she told me, 'kicking in all the doors and everything.'

Although she never told me the cause of their row, I believe he'd picked a fight with her for producing so many boys and never giving him a girl of his own.

She was begging the nurses to keep me in for longer to ensure that Emma and I were safe. They weren't keen to keep me in hospital any longer than they had to, as they needed the bed for new cases, but they agreed to give me one more day.

A few hours after Mum had gone, Richard turned up, all smiles and charm.

'You ready to come home then?' he asked, picking Emma up and giving her a cuddle. He was always so lovey dovey with Emma. He was never like that with anyone else.

'Yeah,' I said, careful not to let a flicker of my true dread show through as I got Emma's things ready.

As soon as we got back to the house he made it obvious that he was going to do nothing to help Paul and me get rehoused, his only concern being how long it would be before he and I could start having sex again.

'You think you're going to get out of here, don't you?' he taunted me. 'But you ain't going nowhere. I'm never gonna write that fucking letter for you.'

The only way that the council would find us a place would be if we were going to be made homeless, which meant that Richard or Mum had to write a letter saying they were going to be throwing us out onto the street. Richard refused to do it and forbade Mum from doing it either. As long as they said they were happy to house us, the council would not give us anything of our own.

Paul did his best to cope with living with Richard but I could see that if we didn't get a place of our own soon he would be driven away and Emma and I would be left there with Silly Git on our own. I began to wonder if maybe that was Richard's plan. Now he had Emma, why did he need Paul around any more? There were moments when he seemed to believe that Emma was actually his own daughter, as if she was a product of one of those dreadful nights when we had slept together like a married couple.

A health visitor came to see us and not realizing Richard was only my stepfather, she commented how much Emma looked like her granddad. I felt a chill run through me. Even though I knew it wasn't possible she was his, the thought of it made me want to die.

'I can't cope any more, Mum,' I told her once he was out of the house. 'I have to get out of here, you know I do.'

Then Mum did the bravest thing I can remember her doing. Maybe the fact that there was a baby in danger now as well as me made her decide to take a risk. Maybe she could remember the early days when she used to have to take me to the toilet with her in order to protect me from my stepfather. Whatever it was, she wrote the letter for me.

'Get down to the council offices now,' she said, pushing it into my hand, 'as quickly as possible, before he finds out and comes after you. Don't look back, just get on the bus and go.'

All the way there my heart was in my mouth, my eyes swivelling round every corner, terrified that Richard would appear behind me and start a scene, grabbing the letter and dragging me back home by my hair, as I'd seen him do to Mum so many times when we were children. I knew that he was perfectly willing to make scenes in public. I sometimes thought he could kill someone in the middle of the street in broad daylight and no one would have the nerve to do anything about it.

The council acted quickly once they had Mum's letter and we were allocated a flat four weeks later. I still wasn't sure that Richard would allow us to physically leave the house but, to my surprise, he let us move out without making a fuss.

I couldn't believe it. I was actually out of his house for the first time since I was four. How could it all have ended so easily when it had been so hard to escape him for so long? One minute I was telling myself it was too good to be true, that it must be a trap of some sort, the next I was overwhelmed with excitement at the thought that my ordeal might finally be over and that now I could live in peace with a man who loved me and take care of my beautiful baby.

The flat was up about eighty stairs, with views over the whole town. On our first night there Emma slept through the night for the first time ever, as if she instinctively knew that she could now relax. The neighbours were all very friendly, although God knows what they were up to. The smells coming through the walls from next door had me high most of the time. I was so innocent that when they came knocking on the door asking for scales I thought they were planning to do a bit of cooking, not weighing up 'gear' to sell. Eventually the police surrounded the block and told us all to stay in our flats. There was then a lot of shouting and banging before they drove off with my neighbours and life went back to normal. It might not have sounded like the ideal place to be bringing up a baby, but to me it seemed like paradise.

Was the nightmare finally over? Or did Richard have some vile new scheme up his sleeve? After fourteen years with him I should have known the answer to that.

Chapter Eight

I should have known that Richard would never have given up that easily. If he was letting us move into our own flat it was because he had seen a way to work the situation to his advantage. How could I have been so naïve not to have realized? Knowing him as well as I did, why didn't I see what was coming next?

The flat we were given was twenty minutes' drive from Richard and Mum's house and I truly thought I had got far enough away to be safe. I never stood a chance. Paul had a job which meant he left the flat at eight each morning, so every day at nine, after my brothers had gone to school, Richard would turn up at the front door. What could have been better for him? He had Emma and me all to himself with no chance of other family members turning up unannounced to disturb him. He had a flat with a double bed in it and knew Paul wouldn't be back until the afternoon. His reign of terror over me could continue uninterrupted.

Paul knew that Richard dropped in all the time, although he didn't know the half of it. If Richard was still there at a time when Paul might come home early I would slip the chain on the door so he wouldn't walk in on us. When I heard his key in the door I would have time to stop Richard doing whatever he was doing and get to the door to unchain it. By being too terrified and ashamed to tell Paul what was going on, I'd given Richard another weapon with which to control me. Now I wasn't just frightened of what he would do to me and Mum and Emma if I betrayed him, I had Paul to think about as well. It felt as if my head was going to explode with it all.

I tried inviting friends round at the time Richard would be there so that he wouldn't be able to get me on my own, but he would just threaten and insult them and they weren't willing to put up with his rudeness, so he was able to get rid of them within a few minutes.

I tried developing a few techniques of my own, like saving up Emma's feeds until I knew Richard was due to come round, then making him hang about and wait while I made her comfortable, and taking as long as possible about it. The trouble was he always would wait, having nothing else to do, and in the end I would still have to give him what he wanted, so I would just have delayed the inevitable.

After he'd done whatever he wanted, he would sometimes make me go back with him to Mum's house, bringing their beloved granddaughter with me. Later he would bring me back to the flat and make me do it all again before Paul got home. If I tried to hide from him, pretending I wasn't in when he rang the intercom downstairs, he would just kick the main door open and come up anyway; the lock wasn't strong enough to keep him out.

Sometimes I would go to other people's houses, but he would bring my brothers round to help him root me out and to look after Emma while he had his way with me in another room. If there was no answer when he knocked on the door, he would sometimes send them up the fire escape to peer through my patio doors while he came in from the front, like a hunter sending the ferrets in to flush out a rabbit.

When the boys were around we had to act out a charade, with me saying, 'Can you look at such and such for me?' and going into the bedroom or bathroom with him to look at some fictitious problem. He would order them not to move and to stay with Emma till we got back.

Although I loved Paul and I knew he loved me, it was impossible to carry on a normal relationship with so many stresses and such terrible secrets coming between us. By the time he got home from work I would be in such a state I would have to take it out on someone and he was such a kind, patient man he would get it all, without having any idea what he was doing wrong.

In the end I could see no choice but to finish our relationship. I loved him, but I knew that I was ruining his life and I could see no way that things could ever be any different. He was such a good man, always handing over his pay packet and putting up with whatever I said, but perhaps deep down I resented the fact that he wasn't rescuing me. How could he, when he didn't know the trouble I was in? He saw Richard's moods and knew what a terrible influence he was on me, but he had no idea of the abuse that was going on every day while he was out at work.

He begged me not to end it and I felt terrible about doing it, but I couldn't cope with everything that was going on in my head. I wanted to make him hate me so he would go under his own steam and I wouldn't feel so guilty, but it didn't work. Still, I finally convinced him that I was serious and that the relationship had to end.

After that I moved into a flat on my own, which meant that I didn't have to worry about Paul and what I was doing to his head, but also meant that Silly Git had even more unrivalled access to me. To make matters worse, this flat was closer to his home than the first one, only five or ten minutes' drive away. It felt as if I was being reeled back in.

Sometimes my brother Pete would let himself into my flat as well. I would just come home and find him there. At first he would try to pretend that I'd left the door open but eventually he had to own up that he had a key. I felt I had no privacy or independence, but he just laughed my protests off.

Richard made it clear from the first day that the flat was his territory now. If he was sitting in the armchair smoking a cigarette, he would casually tip the ashtray onto the floor and watch as I scurried around clearing it up and assuring him that it wasn't a problem. If I made him a cup of tea he would knock the mug onto the floor and ask for another. After all the years of training I knew better than to show him anything but a cheerful face and endless politeness. If I didn't co-operate I knew I would suffer the consequences.

In the past I'd been frightened that Mum would suffer too, and now there was the added fear that Emma might be used against me. Richard had taken all my boyfriends away from me whenever he chose, what was to stop him taking Emma away if I displeased him? Nothing. I was more trapped than I had ever been.

In an attempt to find some form of freedom, I started spending my milk tokens on bottles of wine. Emma had come off the bottle when she was one, so I didn't need to use them for her any more. I was drinking far too much, but still I couldn't escape. Richard was entirely in control. He told me what time I should be up in the morning, what time I should be home by in the evening and what time I should go to bed. He told me how to decorate the flat and what furniture to buy. If he had any old stuff around the house that he wanted to get rid of he would instruct me to buy it off him. He ruled my life as if I was still a small child and still I had to keep smiling and keep being grateful.

I did at least have one ally at the new flat in my friend Cheryl, who lived nearby. About a year after we moved in I told her everything, which meant she was one of the very few people who knew the truth about what was going on inside that flat. Cheryl had had similar experiences herself and not only did she understand that these things happened, where most people chose to believe they weren't possible, but she also knew how they made you feel, how they left you so terrified that you would rather see your whole life fall to pieces than disobey the orders of your torturer. She had been brave enough to speak out about what had happened to her, but knew better than to try to push me into it before I was ready. She would just try to help in any way she could, coming round and sitting with me if she knew Richard was there and ignoring his insults and abuse as he tried to get rid of her.

'Just having a cup of tea with my friend,' she would blithely reply as he poured out obscenities at her.

Richard and Mum would insist on taking Emma and babysitting her for me whenever they felt like it, whether I wanted them to or not. I didn't want Richard anywhere near my baby, although I didn't actually think he would do her any physical harm. He seemed to put her on a pedestal, as if she was the little daughter he had always wanted and never had. Sometimes I would try to stop him taking her, but I didn't have the strength left to fight.

When Richard and Mum were going down to Southend for a holiday they said they wanted to take Emma with them, because she deserved a holiday. I desperately didn't want her to spend that much time near Richard, but they weren't offering a choice.

'Promise me you'll keep her with you all the time,' I begged Mum, 'that you'll never leave her alone with him.'

'Of course I won't,' she said, as if I was mad to suggest such a thing, as if she hadn't turned a blind eye to the things Richard had done to me throughout my childhood and was still doing now, as if he hadn't beaten her time and time again with no reason and no remorse.

I felt terrible letting Emma go and for the whole five days I didn't step outside the flat, just spent the time frantically decorating Emma's bedroom for when she got back, as if new wallpaper and shiny paint would make everything all right. The future seemed so bleak and I didn't feel I had control over any part of my life, but at least I could control how nice her room was.

I hated some of the things Richard was teaching her, like calling black people 'niggers', which he thought was hysterically funny.

'Your dad has just fucked off,' he would say to her, 'and your mummy is a fat slag and a whore.'

The more I asked him not to say those sorts of things to her, the more he did it. Almost every statement that came out of his mouth was either abusive or racist or offensive in some other way. I felt desperate when I thought that Emma might end up being affected by what she was hearing at this early stage in her life. I wanted even more to run away and hide somewhere with her, but where could I possibly go where my stepfather wouldn't follow? I had no money, and I didn't know anyone outside our area who could have given me shelter. If I went to the police for help he would find out immediately and Emma, Mum and I would all be in danger from the repercussions. Even though I was now an adult and a mother, Richard still seemed invincible and inescapable. If he told me to do something, I automatically obeyed. 'You're an unfit fucking mother,' he would scream at me if I ever tried to argue about anything. 'We could ring social services and have that kid taken off you any time.' My self-esteem was so low by then I actually believed that was true. There were times when I thought about taking both our lives because I couldn't see any other way for us to escape him.

I was teetering right on the edge of insanity, but I did still manage to keep up appearances most of the time for friends and acquaintances. Just like at school, people who didn't know me well thought I was the life and soul of any party, always laughing and joking. Anyone who did know me well, or was around when I'd had too much to drink and allowed my feelings out, however, knew that things were different, although almost none of them knew why.

I met Steve at a party quite soon after leaving Paul and fell in love again, which was not what I had intended to do. Introducing other men into my life had done nothing but complicate things in my head and had always ended up making me miserable when I had to give them up. But something told me this one might be different. I suppose he must have started out being attracted to the extrovert girl with the loud laugh, but he didn't seem to be put off when he found out that I was more complicated than I might at first have seemed. He wasn't like the other men I'd known from round our way. He didn't come from our sort of world and knew nothing of what went on there. He had a job in an office, a career plan, a suit and tie, all of which I liked even if I didn't fully understand them.

I had mixed feelings about letting the relationship go anywhere. I was happy to have met someone like Steve, but also frightened of what would happen to his life if he became involved with us. He came from a good, steady, loving family and wouldn't have dreamed for a second of what was going on behind the closed doors and drawn curtains in our house.

It was about three months before I plucked up the courage to let him be at the flat when my family were around. I knew Richard would dislike him immediately. He would see that he wasn't going to be as easy to intimidate as the others. I knew he would talk about him contemptuously as 'that white-collar wanker' and 'that sissy boy'.

I warned Steve that Richard would take the piss. To my amazement, he didn't seem to be worried. 'I've been called names before,' he told me. 'I think I can take a few more.'

'He really isn't a very nice person,' I insisted.

I didn't dare tell Steve that he had never come across anything like my family, that it might start with a bit of name-calling but if that didn't have the desired effect it would soon escalate to violence. I just couldn't bring myself to explain any more.

Initially, though, Richard was alright to Steve, just going through the mock strict father routine.

'Hope your intentions towards my daughter are good.'

'Yes, very good,' Steve replied, innocently.

Richard then came out into the kitchen and told me what he really thought and I went back into the living room in tears, telling Steve that my dad didn't like him. It still didn't seem to bother him that much. It was as if he just thought I was being over-sensitive about everything.

A few weeks later when my stepdad came round to my house Steve was greeted with: 'Oh fucking hell, not you again!'

Silly Git's behaviour was following its predictable pattern, but Steve didn't seem to be willing to let it get to him. He remained resolutely polite and obliging when asked to help lay patios or give the family a lift to watch the boys in a boxing match. Paul warned him not to do them too many favours or he would be sucked in, and sure enough, the first time Steve said he wasn't able to give Richard a hand with something because he was going to the football, all pretence at being friendly ended. But still I couldn't bring myself to explain to Steve the full extent of Silly Git's hold over me. I did, however, tell him that Richard wasn't my real dad, something I had told hardly anyone before.

One of the nice things about Steve is the open relationship he has with his own parents. He tells them everything. In this case, however, his openness had just the sort of effect that I had dreaded. Richard took to ringing Steve's parents and telling them what he thought of their son and me and threatening all sorts of violence. They weren't the sort of people to put up with that kind of rudeness and aggression without responding and in one of these conversations his mum came to my defence.

'She's not even your real daughter and you're talking about her as if she's some slag!' she shouted at him down the phone.

Richard was immediately onto me, demanding to know who else I'd told this secret to, and as usual he managed to make me feel guilty.

One thing I was pleased about, though, was that Steve and Paul got on well right from the start, even though Richard tried to set them against one another.

'You lot make me sick,' he said when he came round once and found them together. Paul had come to collect Emma and Steve was waiting to take me out. 'He's a cunt and you're just sitting there while he's shagging your missus,' he said to Paul. 'Are you going to let him get away with that?'

'She's not my missus,' Paul pointed out, perfectly reasonably. 'I've got a girlfriend.'

Richard swung round and raised his fist in Steve's face. 'If I see you again I'll fucking lift you.'

'You won't do that,' Steve had said, 'because then I'd just go to the police.'

'I'd be willing to do time for you,' Silly Git sneered, and we all suspected that was true.

If he'd had his way he would have had them both fighting it out with their fists like me and my cousin or Mum and her friends, but they didn't rise to his bait and together their good natures and good sense were too much for him.

If he'd had a choice I think he would have liked to have had Paul back and got rid of Steve. Paul came from our area and Richard knew better how to manipulate him. With Steve he could never be sure how to act in order to get the upper hand.

My head felt as if it would burst with all the different stresses and strains and sometimes Steve would wonder why I was so moody. There was one weekend when he took me down to the coast to stay in a hotel and go clubbing and shopping and we had a really great time. It was so romantic, with drinks in the car and a red rose for me. On the way back home on the Sunday night I started to think about how the weekend was now over and Silly Git would be round again on Monday morning. The thought dragged my spirits down and I just wasn't able to keep my good mood going. I couldn't even pretend to be enjoying myself any more. Steve was hurt and angry that I was being such a cow after he'd done so much for me, but there was no way I could explain to him why my spirits had so suddenly deserted me without telling him everything. The first few inches of the wedge that always came between me and people I cared about had made themselves felt.

Steve did know that I was frightened of Richard, even though he didn't understand completely why, and to please me he would agree to meet me in his car or would come round late in the evenings and leave early in the mornings, just to avoid bumping into him. We developed a code by which I would leave an upstairs light on in a window if Richard was in the flat when Steve was due to visit, and he would know not to come back until the light went out.

Steve was willing to put up with it all up to a point but, because I couldn't tell him the whole story, he eventually found it too much and we split up. I heard the news from Steve's dad when I phoned to talk to Steve and was told that he didn't want to speak to me any more.

Yet again my stepdad had ruined my chances of happiness with a good man and another layer was added to my despair.

This time, however, there must have been some stronger forces at work, because Steve came round to see me again after about six months, during which time his friends had got fed up with hearing him talking about me. He was shocked by the sight of me. During that short time I'd developed an eating disorder and become stick thin. I'd become aggressive and hated the whole world. I didn't care who I upset. I'd lost all self-respect. I suppose my family were finally turning me into someone like themselves.

I was fed up with falling in love with people and having them ripped away from me and Steve and I couldn't decide whether we wanted to stay together now or not. In the end we decided to do a test. We ripped up dozens of little bits of paper, writing 'yes' on half of them and 'no' on the other half. We then put them all into Steve's woolly hat and agreed that we would abide by whichever answer came out first.

The first piece of paper said 'yes'.

'Best of three?' we both said simultaneously.

The first three were all yeses, as were the three after that. Wondering if we had made a mistake, we checked all the others, both of us in tears, and the nos were all still there, but something or someone seemed to be telling us that we were meant to be together.

Anxious to avoid Richard at all costs, we took to living in Steve's car all the time we were together, eating our meals in McDonald's and using the toilets in service stations. I even had a newspaper that I'd cut two eye-holes in, so that I would hold over my face as we drove around in case anyone saw us. It was hardly a conventional relationship.

I don't know what finally gave me the strength to stand up to the man who had been bullying me all my life. Maybe it was because he had succeeded in making me almost as hard as himself, or perhaps it was having Steve and his family as an example of how good life could be if you could live free of fear. Whatever it was that triggered it, just after my twenty-first birthday, seventeen years after social services sent me back to 'that hell-hole', I decided I'd had enough. Maybe it was because Emma was getting closer to the age I was when Richard first started abusing me, or maybe I had just reached a point where I couldn't take any more without cracking up. I was beginning to have dreams in which I'd turned into a lonely old woman because no one had ever been allowed to get close to me, and sometimes I would imagine that Emma and I were dead, just because I couldn't think of any other way out of the situation. It seemed that it was worth one last try to break free of Richard before giving up once and for all.

To begin with, I started to find the nerve to defy him in tiny ways, ways that no one else would ever have noticed but which were huge acts of courage for me. He and Mum idolized Emma, always wanting to have her up at their house and taking her whenever they wanted, regardless of whether I wanted it or not. Their house had become like a shrine to her; Richard had even erected a swing for her in the garden. All day he and Mum would be playing with her and I would sit there, glowering at them, trying to make it as unpleasant for them as possible.

Eventually, one day when Richard came round he said, 'From now on I'm picking Emma up on her own. I don't want your miserable fucking face around our house no more.'

I realized my plan had backfired badly. From then on he just came and took Emma, leaving me alone to think dark thoughts until he decided to bring her back to me.

Then one morning, I thought, 'She's my daughter and you're not having her.'

I was waiting in the flat with her when he arrived, muttering over and over to myself and trying to stoke up my courage as I went to the door. I opened it a crack, keeping my foot against it so he couldn't just walk in as he usually did. If I'd kept it closed he would just have kicked it in – at least this way I felt I stood a chance of running past him if he turned nasty.

'Is Emma ready?' he asked.

'No.'

'What?' He was obviously so shocked to have me talk back to him that he couldn't take in what I'd said. 'Better get her ready then.'

'No,' I said, hardly able to breathe with fear. 'I'm not getting her ready.'

'Get her ready!' he screamed, his face turning bright red as he shouted and spat. 'You've got fifteen minutes. I'll be waiting in the car for her.'

He knew I didn't have a phone, so as long as he didn't let me out of the flat he could come back in for Emma whenever he was ready. He'd also told me countless times how I had 'an eggbox front door' which was only designed to be an interior door and could easily be kicked in.

'You see the plastic filling round these windows?' he'd said once. 'It's only council stuff. All I need to do is take that out and the panes will just pop out.'

It was true that he always seemed to be able to get into the house whenever he wanted to. Once I had thought I was in there on my own and turned round to find him standing behind the curtains, just waiting, because I'd left the patio door unlocked.

Now he strode back out to the car, no doubt confident that he'd nipped my pathetic little rebellion in the bud and that I would be meekly getting Emma ready for him when he returned.

I closed the door quickly and tried to keep calm, breathing deeply and fighting the urge to play safe and give in. I was committed now. I would get a punishment anyway for answering him back. I was going to have to press on, whatever the consequences.

I quickly ran through the options in my mind. It was no good attempting to get out of the back door because that was where he would be parked. My best bet was to be ready at the door when he came back so I could run out the moment he barged in. I was more likely to be safe outside on the street than trapped inside the flat. He wouldn't be afraid to make a scene and smack me about, but he probably wouldn't take it too far in public, especially if I had Emma with me. He would be concentrating on trying to get me back indoors where he would have time to do as much damage as he wanted.

On the kitchen worktop behind the door I'd laid out a carving knife, a Stanley knife and a hammer. I was prepared to use any one of them if necessary. If I killed him it would only mean going to prison, which couldn't be any worse than the life I was already living.

I quickly dressed Emma so that we would be ready to make a run for it when the time came.

Fifteen minutes later Richard was back and banging on the door. I was surprised he didn't just kick it straight in, but maybe the few minutes he had had to gather his thoughts meant that he was keeping control of his temper. Maybe he realized I was serious this time and that he would have to be careful if he wasn't to blow the seventeen years of training me and breaking my spirit.

I was shaking all over and thought I was going to throw up with fear. I put Emma behind me and opened the door a crack again.

'Get Emma out here now,' he ordered.

'You won't be seeing her again,' I told him, my voice trembling uncontrollably.

He ranted and raved, saying he was going to get Mum to sort me out and that he was going to kill me when she'd finished with me, but he didn't force his way into the flat, which surprised me.

'Emma can easily be made to disappear, you know,' he warned. 'You can't watch her every minute of the day. One day you'll look away for a second and she'll be gone.'

I shut the door while he was still yelling about smashing the windows in. I waited for the sound of splintering wood as his foot came through the door, but it never came. It was as if he wasn't sure what to do next. Once he had finished shouting there was just silence.

When I was sure he'd gone I went to a neighbour's house and stayed there until late that night, telling them everything. In one way it felt good to be talking openly about my private nightmare, but at the same time I was still terrified that Richard would find out I had let our secret out of the bag. Eventually I felt it was safe to go home again.

My neighbours gave me a walkie-talkie and promised that if they saw his car or any member of the family approaching they would buzz me and I should grab Emma and run to their flat.

Shortly after Steve and I got back together I told him what I'd done and he bought me a mobile phone and told me that I should call the police if Richard tried to get near me. I was glad to have the phone, but I knew I would never ring the police. If I did that the retribution would be too terrible to contemplate. I'd seen what had happened to other people who had informed on my stepfather and I wasn't ready to go that far yet. At the moment this was still just between him and me.

Everything was quiet for a few days. I felt much the same way a soldier in the front line must feel, waiting for the enemy to attack and never knowing when it's going to come or from what direction. I tried to make life seem normal so as not to stress Emma, but I spent most of my time round with my neighbours as they tried to feed me up a bit.

One afternoon a friend came round with her daughter, who had just started crawling. It was a warm day. 'Let's sit outside,' she suggested, 'get a bit of sun.'

Not having heard anything from Richard for a while and being with someone friendly made me feel safer than usual and I agreed. We took a couple of chairs and sat just outside the door. I had my back to it, so I could see the entrance to my flat, and was talking to my friend as the kids played around at our feet.

Suddenly she turned white.

'What's wrong?' I asked.

'Your dad,' she said, her voice trembling, 'he's just picked up Emma and walked into the flat.'

I couldn't believe it. How could that have happened in just a few seconds with us sitting right there? Along with the fear that I felt rising inside me, a surge of anger roared up at the thought of him taking my baby.

'Go home quickly,' I told her, and she knew from my voice I was serious. She scooped up her child and hurried away. As I went inside I wedged the door curtain into the door to keep it open.

Richard was standing in the kitchen with Emma in his arms, just waiting for me.

'Give her to me and get out,' I said.

'I told you you'd have to watch her all the time,' he taunted. 'This is how easily I can get to her.'

I picked up the Stanley knife from the side where I'd left it.

'Give her to me now!' I screamed.

'I'm taking her,' he sneered. 'There's nothing you can do to stop me. If you try, I'll be contacting social services and telling them what a bad mother you are.'

'Give her to me!' I screamed, refusing to allow myself to be intimidated any more.

He just smiled.

'Give her to me or I'm calling the police!'

Still he didn't move and I stormed back outside, relieved to be out from under the same roof as him, but frantic with worry that he might just walk away with Emma and there would be nothing I could do to stop him. I didn't have the phone with me and I'm not sure I could have dialled the number anyway, the way my fingers were trembling.

'Someone call the police!' I screamed for all to hear. 'He's taking my baby! Call the police!'

Suddenly he was beside me, yelling and swearing at me. But at least he had put Emma down.

'I'm gonna get you,' he repeated over and over, and I thought he was going to hit me, but I didn't care. What would one more beating matter after so many? This time I kept shouting back.

To my amazement, there was a look in his eyes I'd never seen before, as if he was worried. In seventeen years I'd never stood up to him, never challenged him seriously, and he wasn't sure where to go next. He had already used every weapon in his arsenal. There was nothing that he hadn't done to me already and I had survived it all. If he wanted to shut me up now, he was going to have to kill me.

The neighbours were beginning to come out of their doors to see what all the fuss was about. They too seemed to be emboldened by me taking a stand against Richard. It felt as if the tide was finally turning. He obviously wasn't sure if the police had been called or not and so, after one last bravura rant, he turned and left.

I was boiling with anger and I needed to let it out somehow. 'Please,' I said to a neighbour, 'take Emma for a few minutes.' The woman nodded, seeing that I was almost out of my head with rage, and picked Emma up, hurrying her away from the scene.

I stormed back into the flat and started smashing everything in sight, hurling plates and cups and glasses and ornaments to the floor, feeling better with every explosion of breaking china. I wanted to throw out everything Richard had ever touched or sold me or given me. I even managed to heave the three-piece suite he had made me buy off him out into the street – God knows how I found the strength, because it had taken several people hours of pushing and shoving to get it in through the door in the first place. But having been suppressed for so many years, my anger now roared out of me like a tornado, giving me super strength, and there was no point in trying to stop it until it had spent its force.

Eventually I had nothing left to break and I subsided onto the stairs to get my breath before going to my neighbour's to retrieve Emma and bring her back to what was left of our home.

From that day onwards I spent my whole time hiding in my bedroom or in the neighbour's flat, or sitting in Steve's car. I kept all the curtains shut and the doors locked, with knives nearby in case Richard battered his way in and I had to protect Emma. I started sleeping with a carving knife under the bed, just like Mum. Even though Steve had changed all the locks on the doors, I still didn't feel safe. I had seen how Richard would just smash his way into people's houses and I couldn't see how a few flimsy locks were going to be able to keep him out if he was determined to come for us.

After a few days the neighbours started complaining about all my furniture sitting outside and I realized I couldn't just leave it there. It was when three blokes tried to get it back in that we realized just how powerful my anger must have been! Now that anger had subsided I could hardly lift the stuff. I still didn't want anything of Richard's in the flat and started asking around to see if anyone else wanted any of it. Whatever offers people made I accepted, just to get rid of it all.

Sometimes Richard would park outside the flat in his car, beeping the horn for hours on end just to let me know he was still out there and would never go away. The noise must have driven the neighbours mad, but they all knew better than to try to stop him.

Every sound was threatening and it was hard to sleep. When I did drop off I was attacked by dreams of stabbing and shooting Richard and him getting back up and coming for me over and over again, like some invincible zombie in a horror film.

I was so on edge my relationship with Steve was almost impossible. I couldn't bring myself to respond to his advances in bed, even though I loved him, and he was becoming increasingly frustrated by my inability to give any rational explanation for my behaviour. He was trying to understand what was going on in my head, but he lacked the information that would have made the picture clear. He knew that Richard was a nasty, bullying piece of work, but he couldn't understand why I allowed him to terrorize me in the way that he did. Nor could he understand why it had to affect *our* relationship so badly.

Three weeks after the confrontation with my stepdad I realized that I was going to lose Steve, exactly as I'd lost Paul, if I didn't do something positive about it.

I had discovered I was pregnant again and I couldn't face the idea of Richard defiling another of my pregnancies with his sordid demands. I just wanted us to be a normal family with Emma and the new baby, and I knew that if Steve went I would have no protection against Richard when he eventually decided to come back for me. As my pregnancy progressed I would become more vulnerable and once I was looking after two small children I would stand almost no chance of keeping him at bay. I had to do something now.

Chapter Nine

It was two o'clock in the morning and Steve had finally reached the end of his tether. I was about to lose everything I loved again. If I didn't do something to save the situation now I would spend the rest of my life alone and enslaved. I would never be able to break the cycle.

All I had to do was tell Steve the truth, but I just couldn't bring myself to speak the words. It should have been so easy to do, but it was as if a part of my brain was paralysed, refusing to say the words that needed saying, to tell the story that would explain everything to the one person who could help me to escape. There had been so many secrets locked up inside my head for so many years that I'd lost the ability to say what I wanted, even when my happiness and the happiness of the two people I loved most in the world depended on it.

I felt frightened, guilty and embarrassed, all at the same time. I wanted to tell Steve everything, but I was afraid of the possible consequences. It seemed to me that he would be unable to understand why I was so frightened, that he would refuse to keep the secrets, that he would want to go to the authorities and seek revenge, and then we would all be in danger.

'It's not you,' I kept assuring him. 'It's not you.'

'So what is it?' he wanted to know, his anger and frustration at our lack of lovemaking made worse by tiredness. He was such a kind and patient man and I was driving him away, ruining his life just like I'd ruined my other boyfriends', and just like I was ruining my baby's. It seemed that anyone who came close to me was immediately sucked into my terrible world of secrets and pain and fear. I had to do something to stop Steve from deciding that there was no future for us, to stop the relationship crumbling away to nothing, leaving Emma and me totally alone and vulnerable once more. I had to make him understand what had happened to me, why it seemed as if I was losing my mind, but I could no more find the words than jump from an aeroplane without a parachute. It was no good, I told myself, I was going to have to make the jump, I couldn't put it off any longer.

'There's something I have to tell you…' I said, but as I opened my mouth I saw all the terrifying ramifications of what I was about to tell him and my nerve deserted me again. 'I've got to get Cheryl!'

'What do you mean?' He couldn't believe what he was hearing. It must have seemed as though he was living with a total madwoman.

I didn't stop to explain any more, I just ran out of the flat in my dressing-gown, leaving him open-mouthed and confused at the window as I stumbled tearfully down the road to Cheryl's house and hammered on the door to wake her up.

'What is it?' Cheryl's head popped out of the window upstairs. I could hear her husband's sleepy voice in the background asking what was going on.

'Is she alright?' I heard him say.

'I really need you,' I called up, my throat so tight I was choking on the words as I fought back the hysteria. 'You're going to have to come with me.'

Cheryl probably wasn't too thrilled at being woken up and dragged out into the cold night, but she was the only person in the world who really understood what was wrong with me.

She bustled back across the road with me, tying up her dressing-gown cord as she went, probably eager to get me back indoors before I woke the rest of the street up. She was such a good friend I knew she would do whatever I asked of her without hesitation. I'd always been lucky with my friends – the ones I was allowed to keep.

Now I knew there was no going back. I had made the jump from the plane and was plummeting towards the earth. Steve was going to find out everything over the next few hours.

I was already regretting taking the plunge. Steve was such a straightforward bloke. Until he met me his answer to anything like this would just have been to go to the police and report it, but in my world things were far more complicated than that. I was so frightened I wouldn't be able to explain to him how important it was that he guarded my secret as closely as I had guarded it all these years. I knew how much it was going to hurt him and I wasn't sure he would be able to control his anger. I was terrified of what he would do and what the consequences would be.

He was waiting for us in the front room. His anger had subsided now that Cheryl was there, just leaving the puzzlement and an air of tension as he waited to find out once and for all what was going on. He must have known that he was about to discover something bad and it must have made him nervous. What secret could be so terrible that I had allowed it to almost drive us apart when we loved each other so much?

I'd already told Steve a bit about what had happened to Cheryl when she was a child, probably because I was trying to edge him towards understanding my world even before I was ready to tell him the truth, but I don't know if he had completely believed it. People who have had safe, protected and loving childhoods find it almost impossible to believe what goes on in the sort of homes Cheryl and I come from. It takes them time to be able to imagine the sorts of horrors that are forced on children like us and even once they accept them as true I think they push them to the back of their minds. There are lots of things we all push to the backs of our minds, aren't there?

I put on the kettle and made us all a cup of tea – it's my answer to everything. I've always been a right old teapot. Also, the ritual of sipping from mugs would help to distract us from what we were going to have to talk about and it was only polite to offer poor Cheryl some hospitality after dragging her out of bed to do my dirty work for me. Emma was asleep in her cot, unaware of anything.

Eventually Cheryl and I sat on the sofa together with our mugs of hot tea, huddled like small children, while Steve paced round and round the room, unable to sit still as he waited to hear the explanation for everything that was going wrong in his life.

'Listen, Steve,' Cheryl started. 'I know you know what happened to me when I was a kid.'

He didn't answer. I could see that he was concentrating hard, trying to take in every word she said, making sure he understood it and didn't miss anything.

'Well, the same thing happened to Jane with her dad.'

'With Richard?'

You could almost see the words sinking into his mind, taking shape, conjuring up images almost too horrible to bear.

'When did this happen then?' he asked, his voice shaking.

'From when she was four,' Cheryl said.

'Until when?'

'About two weeks ago.'

Steve paced faster as he thought about the life I'd been forced to lead while he'd been out at work. Cheryl kept talking, although I'm sure most of her words must have been washing over Steve by that stage, like trying to empty a bucket of water into a narrow bottle all at once. I sat hunched beside her, every muscle trembling, my mug and cigarette shaking in my hands as I rocked rhythmically back and forth, as I so often did.

'I knew it,' he exploded once the truth had sunk in. 'I fucking knew it.'

'What do you mean?' I wanted to know.

'Ever since I met you I've been getting these images of you and him in my head and I've always thought to myself, "You sick git!" But I never imagined anything like this.'

Cheryl put her arm around my shoulders to try to calm my shaking.

From being gob-smacked Steve became furious, shouting and raging around the room.

'Stop being angry!' I screamed, putting my hands over my ears. 'You're making me feel like I've done something wrong. This is why I didn't want to tell you!'

Steve didn't want to know the details, but he couldn't stop himself from asking. As he heard them, and fitted them in with the things he already knew about my family, I could tell that he had grasped the full horror of the situation. He could see that there was no way we could put right what had happened in the past, but that we had to think of ways to make the future better.

Once he'd got over the shock, his first thought was that we had to go to the police. I had to convince him that I truly didn't want him to do anything about it and wasn't prepared to go to the police or do anything else that would aggravate the situation.

After that, his only thought was that he had to get me away from the area. We decided to make a run for it, taking Emma with us and not telling anyone where we were going, not even Paul. It was going to be a hard thing to do, leaving friends and people who had been good to us without even saying goodbye, but we couldn't take the risk of my stepfather going after someone he believed knew where we were. If he thought for a moment anyone had an address for us, he would beat them mercilessly until he got it out of them. Everyone knew that his rages were uncontrollable when anyone tried to stand up to him or frustrate him. It was even more urgent that we got away soon because I wanted to be gone before my family knew anything about my new pregnancy. I wanted my new baby's life to be completely untainted by them.

The morning after he learned the truth Steve got up at the normal time, no longer willing to wake up before dawn in order to get away unseen. It was as if the gloves had finally come off. He was still in shock when he got into his car and drove to work. A few streets away he found himself in traffic and spotted his mum in the car in front. He flashed her frantically until she pulled over. Collapsing into tears, he told her the whole story.

'We're gonna have to move from the area quick time,' he said.

'Whatever you need, we'll help with,' she told him, 'anything we can do.'

I'd known that Steve would have to tell his parents about what had happened to me, because that was the sort of relationship he had with them. But even that was hard because although Steve's dad was a tough man, neither of his parents were young and I knew what my stepfather was like with his threatening phone calls, his notes through the door and the hours he would spend sitting in the Cortina outside people's houses flashing his lights onto the windows and beeping his horn over and over again. He knew how to make people aware that they weren't safe anywhere, especially in their own homes. He was always a master at making people's lives a misery.

I trusted Steve's parents, but I was terrified by the thought of anyone else knowing about our plans. The more people who knew, the greater the danger that word would get back to my stepdad and the more certain it would be that he would take it out on me when he found me. It had always been his golden rule, right from the first moment when he pressed the carving knife against my throat, that no one must ever know what went on between us when we were alone or he would kill me and Mum. Nothing he'd done in the seventeen years since then had given me any reason to doubt him. If he found out that I had talked before we managed to get away from the area, the consequences were unthinkable.

I was particularly careful to keep everything from Cheryl, because for some time she had been the one who was most likely to get trouble from Richard because of the way in which she had protected me. Even though she was as scared of him as everyone else, she had always felt she had something over him because she knew what he was up to with me, and that had given her the courage to face him down.

Paul had been telling Steve he should take Emma and me away from the area for some time. Although he would miss seeing his daughter, he had realized that there was no other way out for us. I felt terrible at the thought of not keeping in contact with him, but I knew I couldn't, because Richard and my brothers would be putting pressure on him to tell them where I was. I just hoped that he would understand why.

I would have to cut off all my friends in just the same way. I couldn't take the chance of them being intimidated into giving us away. If any of them stored my new number in their mobile phones, for instance, and those phones fell into unfriendly hands, I would soon start receiving abusive calls and it wouldn't be long before I was getting visits again. I had to cut myself off completely.

Richard didn't make direct contact with me for several weeks after I confronted him, which gave us a chance to lay our plans, but that didn't mean he wasn't still a presence in my life, hovering threateningly in the background, letting me know that he could reappear in my life whenever he decided. The Cortina would often be in the street outside the flat, the horn going and going and going, making me want to scream.

One evening Steve went out to buy a kebab and chips, since I was still too scared to even go into the kitchen to cook in case Richard barged in through the back door. He was ages coming back and I began to worry as I hid in the bedroom. When he did eventually reappear, he was shaking like a leaf. He climbed out of the car, dragging our supper after him, ripping the bag so that there were kebab and chips falling all over the place. He had taken to carrying a hammer under his seat in case Richard had ever got him cornered in the street, and he held it in his other hand. As he stumbled towards the flats he trod on some of the fallen food, skidded and fell heavily on the steps. By the time he finally got into the flat he was gasping for breath, almost overcome with adrenaline.

'He spotted me when I got back in the car,' he said. 'He drew up beside me as I parked, so I couldn't get away, and indicated he was going to park because he wanted to have it out. When he got out of the car I just stood on the horn, over and over. I wanted to attract your attention and bring everyone else to their windows. I couldn't get my car window open because the handle was broken, so I was shouting through the glass at him, pointing at the faces: "See all this? Everyone knows about you!" There was a real look of panic on his face, but he was still coming at me. I didn't hang about. I could see what he had in mind. I took off, with him after me. I wanted to draw him away from the area, so he wouldn't go in looking for you. I went up towards the police station and he turned off. I was afraid he was coming back here, so I did a U-turn in the road and then he was behind me again. I slowed right down to ten miles an hour and he just drove off.'

Another morning we woke up to find the tyres on Steve's car had been let down and so we had to start hiding it in other streets. Life obviously couldn't go on like this.

One day there was a knock at the door and I found my brother Dan there. I hadn't seen him since I'd taken my stand against Richard. He must have been about fourteen by then.

'Alright, Dan?' I said.

'Dad wants all his jewellery back,' he told me.

'All right then, mate,' I said, holding no grudge against him. 'Do you want to come in while I get it?'

He shook his head and his eyes went to the ground. I could tell that Silly Git must be watching from his car somewhere. As I was keen to get rid of anything that had anything to do with him, I happily gathered up everything he or Mum had ever given me for birthdays or Christmases.

'Tell him he can keep the lot,' I said as I handed it back, 'because I don't want it anyway.' I was surprised at my own courage in being so mouthy.

'I really miss you,' Dan mumbled.

'I still love you, Dan,' I said, giving him a kiss and a cuddle. 'I miss you, too, and I'm sorry about everything, but it's not my fault.'

I could see he was holding back the tears. He wouldn't want his father to see he had been crying when he got back to the car.

Even though we were laying plans to escape from the area, Steve was still all for going to the police, believing that Richard only got away with the things he did because everyone was afraid to stand up to him. He tried his hardest to convince me, but he could see that I was not in a fit state to do anything like that. We were going to have to slip away in the night if we wanted to build any sort of normal life for ourselves and the children. We were going to have to accept that, like it or not, my stepfather had succeeded in driving us away from our home and our friends.

But how do you choose where to live when you can go virtually anywhere? And how would we find a house we could afford? It was bound to take a few weeks to arrange. The one stipulation was that Steve needed to be within about three-quarters of an hour's drive of his work, but that covered a huge area. The only places I didn't want to go were anywhere that I'd been to with my stepdad, like the DIY stores he was always taking me to in other towns. I didn't want to go anywhere where there was the slightest chance I might bump into him when I was out shopping.

So we were aiming to find a place that I'd never heard of and where you could get the cheapest houses possible, since Steve wasn't earning all that much. I had actually been in council housing long enough to qualify for help with buying a property and could have got £14,000, which would have helped Steve a lot, but we couldn't take the risk of anyone in the council knowing where we'd gone. We needed to disappear completely, so we had to sort the house out on our own.

Buying your first property is a big enough step for any young couple without having to do it under this sort of pressure. Every delay at the solicitor's or the estate agent's sent us into a whirl of panic. They must have thought they were dealing with mad people. They all kept trying to reassure us that they bought and sold properties for people all the time and knew what they were doing, and we kept trying to convince them that they had no idea how important it was that the transaction went through quickly.

One of the estate agents we went to took us to a place that was on the market for less than £50,000. It was a repossession and the people who'd lost it had taken their revenge by trashing the place before they left, even down to smearing the walls with excrement. It was grim, but at least it would be a home of our own once we'd managed to clean it up. I was used to cleaning places up anyway – the flat the council had given me when I first managed to get away from home had been in an even worse state – and we were grateful to get anything. I also knew a lot about doing places up, having watched my stepdad do it so many times, and about keeping them nice, having been his domestic slave for so many years. Steve's dad, being a painter and decorator, promised to help us to make the place habitable.

When the deal was finally done and we had the keys to our new home, we had to move in the middle of the night to be sure Richard wouldn't turn up halfway through and create a scene. Even though we didn't have much stuff it was still going to take an hour or two to get everything into the van and we couldn't risk someone seeing us and ringing him. I'd already given a lot of things away to friends and neighbours, telling them that I was buying new and didn't need any of it any more. I especially didn't want to take anything to do with Richard, anything he'd sold me or even touched, particularly the bed, which held so many terrible memories. I'd even given away the carpets, since all the flats in the block were the same size and shape. For the final few days before the move I'd been sitting on bare boards in garden chairs, praying Richard wouldn't turn up and see what I was up to.

Steve's dad and some of his friends came round at midnight to help and even though we tried to be quiet, the activity brought the neighbours out, lights flickering on all over the block and people asking why we hadn't told them we were going. I couldn't give them any explanation, which was hard, as some of them had been very friendly to us in the past. I was just frantic to get away before Richard turned up to stop us, stuffing everything into the van and fielding the questions of curious, offended neighbours with helpless shrugs. Emma had already gone to stay with Steve's mum. We were going to spend the rest of the night at their house before going on to our new home at first light.

The following morning we set out early in the van, taking Emma with us. Steve's dad came too, to help with the moving in. It felt good to be finally leaving the area, even if it did mean moving into a house that smelled so bad we all had to eat outside in the garden for the first few days. We spent every waking hour scrubbing and scraping, but finally the place was habitable.

It must have taken a fantastic amount of courage for Steve to decide to move to an area he didn't know, cutting himself off from many of his friends and relatives in order to give me and Emma a safe home and taking on the whole financial burden.

On top of all that he had to deal with my fragile state of mind. On the one hand I was relieved to finally be away from my family, but at the same time I was still looking over my shoulder the whole time, expecting Silly Git to turn up at any moment. Every time the phone rang I was sure he had tracked down my number. Every time I saw a Cortina my blood would freeze and the familiar sense of panic would rise inside me. I had a small child to care for and a pregnancy to deal with, at the same time as trying to hang on to my sanity. I can't have been easy to live with.

Although it was an enormous relief to be free from Richard, I missed my brothers and my friends. I felt as if I had abandoned the boys and wanted them to know that I still loved them and that it wasn't them I was hiding from. A few days after going I rang their headmistress and explained a bit about what had happened.

'I just want to talk to them,' I said, 'so I can tell them that I haven't forgotten them. Can you ask them to come to your office after school and I'll ring at three-thirty. Please don't tell them why you want to see them.'

She was very understanding and said she would do what she could. I waited by the phone until the exact moment that I'd said I would call and then dialled with trembling fingers.

'I'm so sorry, Jane,' the headmistress said, 'because you asked me not to tell them why I wanted them in the office they assumed they were in trouble and ran off the moment school finished.'

I felt so sad not to be able to communicate with my brothers. I found myself thinking about them a lot and wondering how they were coping. When it was their birthdays I would buy cards for them, although I never sent them, and thought about them all day. I used to plan how we might be able to get hold of Tom, who seemed to be the most vulnerable one, and bring him to live in safety with us. Steve was quite happy to go along with the plan, but we never worked out how to do it.

Although I was now physically free of Richard, I was still suffering mentally from everything that had happened before, as well as from the ever-present fear that he would track me down and turn up on the doorstep. Sometimes I would resort to drink to try to fight the depression, picking up a couple of bottles of wine after dropping Emma at school in the morning, or I would just stay inside the house for months on end, terrified to step outside.

If you have been a slave all your life, used to being ordered about and abused from the moment you wake up to the moment you go to sleep, it's impossible to adjust to normal life overnight. I had never been free to make my own decisions before and had no idea how to do it. I was like a bird that has been bred in captivity suddenly being released into the wild: I fell apart.

When other people were around I could keep up the pretence of being a carefree, zany person, but I knew I was close to the edge and needed to talk to someone professionally. I kept telling my doctor that I needed help, but she didn't seem to see any urgency in the situation. As far as she was concerned, I was someone who had arrived from nowhere and seemed to be coping. She had no idea of my history and there was never enough time for me to be able to explain fully what I'd been through.

'I'm alright at the moment,' I kept saying, 'but I know I need to sort my head out or it'll all blow up later. I've seen too many people who have fallen to pieces because they haven't dealt with their problems early.'

My doctor just looked puzzled and referred me to a counsellor.

I made an appointment with the woman, but I said I would have to bring Emma along because I couldn't get her looked after at that time.

'Oh that's fine,' the counsellor assured me. 'This meeting is just to get the formalities out of the way and get the names and family tree straight.'

She was a nurse who had just finished a counselling course. When I started telling her what had been happening, her jaw dropped and she looked at Emma.

'So d'you think he could be her dad then?' she asked.

That was the end of the session for me. I didn't feel confident that she knew what she was doing.

But I knew that one day I would have to face my demons once and for all.

Chapter Ten

I had given birth to my second daughter, Sophie, a few months after going into hiding. Richard and Mum had never even known I was pregnant again and I liked the idea that they didn't realize Sophie existed, that she never had to be connected to them in any way.

We were working so hard to create a nice family atmosphere for our girls, but the demons were still at work deep in my head, trying desperately to push me off the rails with the memories and the confusion and the anger and the guilt and everything else that had become entangled in there over the years. As long as I had a small baby to look after, though, I was too busy to really attend to the thoughts and emotions that were cluttering up my mind.

The things I'd told him must have been playing on Steve's mind all the time, however. I know a lot of his friends got fed up with him going on about it when they all went out together and were trying to have a good time.

On the first New Year's morning in our new house, after Steve had had a heavy night's drinking with one of his friends, I came downstairs to find them both looking very furtive. I didn't think it was just because they'd been so drunk the night before, because that wasn't such an unusual event.

'What is it?' I asked.

'Nothing,' Steve assured me, unable to look me in the eye.

The phone rang and the colour seemed to drain from his face. It was his dad, telling us he'd had a call from my mum saying that I had to contact her, that it was really serious.

'What could that be about?' I wondered. 'Maybe she's going to tell me Richard's dead.'

'I'm really sorry, Janey,' Steve said, realizing he had no option but to confess. 'We had a bit to drink last night and we rang your mum and I gave her a piece of my mind.'

'You told her you knew?' I couldn't believe what I was hearing. This was my worst nightmare come true. Now my stepdad would know that I'd told other people, that I'd broken his golden rule. 'You stupid git!'

That call, coming out of the blue, must have been a hell of a shock to my stepdad, when he'd always been so confident that I would never find the nerve to disobey him. We heard through other friends of Steve's, who still lived in the old neighbourhood, that my mum was going round all the houses the next day saying that I was making accusations against my father (they were still keeping up the pretence that he was not my stepfather) and that they wanted to make sure no one said anything.

'Janey's spreading rumours,' she was telling them, 'and we don't want to hear anyone talking about them.'

I knew that anyone who had had a visit from my mum would be anxious not to do anything to upset her or my stepdad.

When my anger at Steve had subsided enough for me to be able to talk straight, I gave Mum a ring, my heart thumping, wondering what would happen next.

'Is it true?' she asked.

'Is what true?'

'You know what. Is it true?'

'Yeah.'

'Why didn't you tell me?'

'You wouldn't have believed me, and if you had, he would have ended up killing both of us. Where is he now?'

'He's out. He's going fucking mad. He's looking for the person who made the call.'

'He knows who made the call,' I pointed out. 'He's just looking for an excuse to do some damage. Don't ever let on that you believe it's true.'

For years after that I had dreams that the police had come knocking on my door to tell me that they'd found my mother dead in a pool of blood because she'd let Richard know that she believed what I'd said about him.

Very soon afterwards Richard and Mum moved to the other end of the estate.

From the moment he'd learned the truth, Steve had thought I should go to the police and report what had happened to me. His parents were the same and I had to tell them that it was never going to happen, that I was never going to be able to find the courage to stand up in court and accuse my stepfather openly of the things he'd done to me, that the repercussions would be too terrible. They could all see that they were putting me under more pressure by going on about it, so they stopped, but I knew they still believed it and in my heart I knew they were right.

When I looked at my two girls, I wondered what I would say to them if they came to me one day and told me someone had attacked them. If I said they must go to the police and they turned round and said, 'But you never did', what would I say to them?

It's terrible to know that you should be doing something but not be able to find the courage to do it. It makes you feel bad about yourself every day. Not that I needed any new excuses to feel bad about myself. My relationships with any new friends I made were all going wrong and the pressures were building up. On top of that we had terrible money problems. Steve's salary only just covered the mortgage repayments and there was the cost of the petrol needed to get him to and from work. When Sophie was born, she had to be dressed and equipped completely from car-boot sales or with hand-me-downs from friends and Steve's family. We could hardly afford to feed ourselves properly. For Christmas we were only able to give Emma six *Caspar* videos, which we'd been able to get for a pound each. She was so excited about them that it was one of the best Christmases she ever had, but we felt terrible. 'Another *Caspar* video!' she exclaimed in wonder as she unwrapped each one.

As soon as Sophie was sleeping through the night I took a job as a cleaner to try to help with the money. I would work from seven in the evening to three in the morning, scrubbing toilets and everything else, but the strain, along with everything else, was too much. I had to give it up after a few weeks.

One of the things I was fed up with was all of us having different names. If we were going to be a family, then we should do it properly.

'Let's get married,' I said to Steve one evening and he happily agreed. 'The girls can be our bridesmaids.'

I always found life easier to cope with when I was busy and had things to plan. A wedding was a great distraction from the clouds forming in my brain, even if we couldn't invite most of the people who were important to us, but once it was all over I was back in the same life, with the same problems.

Once Sophie was old enough to start going to play-group, there were a few hours a day when I had nothing else to do other than brood. Although the house we had moved into was nice enough, it was almost exactly the same layout as every council house I had ever had to live in with Silly Git, and when I was inside it I still didn't feel I had really escaped. So many things could trigger a bad memory or a panic attack – something the kids might say or a smell I recognized from my childhood – and pictures would come flooding back, reminding me of the things I'd fought so hard to forget.

Over the next couple of years my drinking grew worse whenever I felt low. Every morning after dropping Emma at school and Sophie at playgroup, I would buy a couple of bottles of wine and another packet of paracetamol, some from this shop, some from that shop, and would spend the morning drinking and staring at the tablets, trying to pluck up the courage to take them and end it all. Every day I would bottle out and just get drunk instead.

I found the drink allowed me to have a cry and feel sorry for myself. When I was stone cold sober I would tell myself that there were plenty of people in the world who were worse off than me and I would force myself to get a grip. Once the wine had taken a hold, however, my grip would loosen, the tears would flow and I would weep for everything that had been taken away from me. I would become convinced that I was ruining everyone's lives, including Steve's and the girls', and that they would all be better off without me.

I regularly considered all the possible methods of suicide and on more than one occasion crossed a busy road with my eyes closed. It seemed as if I had a guardian angel, however, because not only did the traffic miss me, but the various implements I used to try to slash my wrists never seemed to hit the right spot. Sooner or later, though, I was in danger of succeeding and Emma and Sophie would be without a mum.

One day I had all my hair cut off. When Steve left the house in the morning I looked as I always had, with long hair, when he came back in the evening it was all gone and I had shorter hair than him.

'Yeah,' he said, swallowing back his urge to say what he really thought, 'no, I like it. Yeah, it looks great. No, really.' It was a long time before he plucked up the courage to tell me just how shocked he had been by the transformation.

All the strain of propping my failing sanity up was now falling on Steve's shoulders, with a little support from a few friends I had made in our new location.

Steve's parents were always so kind to me, but it must have been a terrible shock to them when their son first brought home a girl from the sort of family background I'd had. I'm sure they were relieved when we split up for six months, but once Steve had made his mind up that I was the one he wanted, they always backed us both up in every way possible and treated me just like a daughter.

Now they were under relentless pressure from my family, who were making threatening phone calls in the night and doing a lot of other stuff they wouldn't tell me because they didn't want to upset me. They were not the sort of people to be easily intimidated, but it was making their lives unpleasant and confirmed that we had made the right decision in not putting that same pressure on anyone else who might have buckled under it.

With Sophie's arrival, there were three people who needed me to get better in order to be able to cope with our family life properly. Finally, after spending a year on the waiting list, I was given an appointment with a clinical psychiatrist at the local mental health centre. She talked to me very nicely, explaining where I was on the scale between depressed and euphoric – and I was pretty near the bottom.

I kept begging her to section me. I just wanted a rest and to be looked after by someone else.

'No.' She shook her head. 'If you didn't have a family then I would, but if I take you away from them there's a danger you'll simply give up.'

Many times when I was in her waiting room over the coming weeks I would hear people crying and screaming because they had been sectioned when they didn't want to be and I was envious of them.

She prescribed me tranquillizers, anti-depressants, vitamins and sleeping pills, some of them so strong they could only be dispensed by the hospital, and referred me on to a psychologist.

'You're a man!' I said when I first walked into his office. Not only was he a man, but he also looked about my own age, which I thought was going to be a bit embarrassing.

'Is that a problem?' he asked.

'I think so. I want a woman. How do I know you aren't doing these things to your own kids?'

'Since you're here, why don't you try me?' he suggested. 'Because it could be a long wait if you ask to go to someone else.'

I did as he suggested and immediately knew that I had found the right person. It was as if a lead weight had been lifted from my shoulders from the first moment I started talking to him. I poured out everything that had happened to me since the age of four, sparing him none of the details, and he listened and understood how I felt. Someone was actually paying attention to me and not getting angry or being shocked or telling me to pull myself together or to go to the police or anything, just listening.

Often as I talked his eyes would start watering up. 'It's me who's meant to be crying,' I would joke, 'not you.'

When I showed him some poems I'd written during my bleakest moments he asked if he could take them home to read as he found it a bit much with me in the room. He later told me that everything I had written was classic for someone who had been through what I had.

Over the coming months he did a brilliant job of making me feel better about myself. For the first time I began to believe that everything that had happened to me hadn't been my own fault and I started to feel my courage growing. I still didn't feel strong enough to go to the police and start the long battle to have Silly Git put away, but a number of things were falling into place in my head. I actually began to think that perhaps I didn't have anything to feel guilty and ashamed about. I truly was the wronged party here.

The psychologist also recommended books for me to read which opened my eyes to the fact that I wasn't alone in the world, there were other people who understood it all. After years of being told that reading meant putting on airs and graces, I was suddenly reading books all the time. It was as if my brain had been starved for years and years and now I had to stuff as many pages into it as possible.

One of the books I read was *A Child Called It* by Dave Pelzer and I was inspired by the way in which he had got his life together after his abused childhood. I knew a lot of people who had read it and said they couldn't believe that everything he had written about his mother was true, but I believed it because I had been there too. I could imagine every single scene that he described.

'You *have* to read this book,' I told my psychologist on my next visit. 'You absolutely have to read it. There must be a school somewhere turning out these people, because they're all the same.'

'What people?' He took the book from me, looking puzzled. 'What do you mean?'

'People who do these things to children. They must all come from the same place. They do all the same things. Everything his mother did I can imagine my stepdad doing.'

It took a year of psychotherapy before I felt able to seriously think of going to the police. You can't overcome a lifetime of fear overnight and I changed my mind a hundred times, but I finally decided I felt strong enough to do what I had always known I should.

'I think I might be able to go to the police about Silly Git,' I told Steve one day.

It was just what he had been hoping to hear. He believed with all his heart that no man should be allowed to get away with those sorts of crimes against a child and he had wanted me to speak out for years.

He and his parents had kept saying things like 'How will you feel if he does it to someone else and you could have stopped him?'

Now Steve went straight to the local police station on my behalf. There they told him that he had to lodge the complaint at the station in the area where the crimes had been committed. He drove straight there. I think he wanted to make sure he got the ball rolling before I had a chance to change my mind. He was right. I changed my mind at hourly intervals from then on, but it was too late to go back now and most of the time I knew I was doing the right thing, even if sometimes the fear became almost too much to bear.

An officer called Marie from the Child Protection Unit came to visit me first. I could see that she was more or less going through the motions and I felt guilty for bothering her. I kept apologizing and saying I was sure there must be better things she could be doing with her time, rescuing children who were in danger now rather than listening to a grown-up complaining about something that happened years ago. I always felt guilty when I watched news programmes about children starving in Africa or losing limbs to landmines, thinking that I really didn't have that much to complain about. Now I kept saying that it wasn't that bad and that kids were probably going through worse all the time. I must have been undermining Marie's confidence in the case with every new thing I said.

Marie asked me if my stepfather had ever been arrested and I said he'd been arrested hundreds of times but he never ended up going to prison because he always intimidated the witnesses and anyone who brought charges against him always withdrew them again under pressure. I could see that she was becoming exasperated and I realized that it did sound like a far-fetched story.

'Pull his file,' I said. 'Then you'll be able to see for yourself.'

By the time she left I think Marie was thinking about just putting my complaint on file and leaving it at that. She had explained very patiently how hard it was for the Crown Prosecution Service to actually prosecute in a case like mine. I wasn't surprised, sure that I must be one of millions who had had terrible things done to them in their childhood, but pleased that I had at least spoken up. As long as my complaint was on record somewhere, I reasoned, Richard would be less likely to get away with the same thing again.

To my surprise Marie came back the very next day, having checked Richard's record.

'I've got something for you,' she said, holding a roll of paper up level with the top of her head. She then allowed it to unravel all the way to the floor. Every inch of it was covered in data about my stepfather.

'That's just his arrests in the last seven years,' she said.

I felt a surge of relief, realizing that someone in authority was actually going to believe what I was saying.

'I think we'd better start again from the beginning, don't you?' Marie said.

We set to work to sort out my memories and build a case that her bosses would be willing to take to court. 'The Crown Prosecution Service will only take this on if they think there's a reasonable chance of winning it,' she warned me.

It wasn't hard remembering the many dreadful things that had happened to me, but it was almost impossible to get them into any sort of coherent order as my mind jumped from one thing to the next. I could see that the more I told Marie, the more confused she became.

'Did he do that to you when you were five or ten?' she would ask. 'Did it go on for a month, a year? When did that happen? How often? How long?'

So often I couldn't give a definite answer and every question sent me off on another babbling stream of consciousness as Marie's pen flew over the page, trying to get it all down in some form that would make sense later. Realizing that there was more than the normal amount of material to sift through, she was forced to bring in a colleague to help her.

In most child abuse cases the abuse only happens for a few years before the child is either saved or the abuser loses interest because their victim matures. Seventeen years was an astonishingly long time to have been systematically abused and made the task far harder than usual as I dredged up one ghastly memory after another.

Marie went to social services to get my file to see whether they had had any idea what was going on and what they might have been doing about it.

'They've lost the file,' she told me over the phone. 'I've told them they've got a week to find it before I send in a team to search properly.'

I could tell how angry she was. She told me it was not the first time this had happened to her in the course of an investigation.

A week later nothing had surfaced and she sent in a team of police to go through every file in the building. They found nothing. Someone had removed every trace of the evidence.

'What does this mean?' I wanted to know.

'It means his defence team will say it would have been impossible for him to have been treating you the way he did because social services were coming round all the time to check that you were alright.'

'But they never came near me that I can remember,' I insisted. 'And even if they had, I would never have had the nerve to tell them what was going on.'

Undaunted, Marie and her colleague continued getting everything they could out of me, until their fingers were aching with the pain of writing.

'We're going to have to stop now,' Marie told me finally. 'We can't put in every last thing he ever did to you or this case will last forever.'

They went away to have the whole sorry story typed up. When they came back with the typescript, Marie was armed with a pair of scissors and a Pritt stick.

'You've got to go through this,' she explained, 'and cut it up and stick it back together in some sort of order so that the lawyers can understand it.'

I tried to do as she said, but I was still having trouble putting things in order.

'The woman who typed this up,' Marie told me as we went through it together, 'has been working in the department for nearly twenty years, but she had to keep leaving the room because she was crying when she was typing up your words.'

'So do you think they'll prosecute him?' I asked.

'Who knows?' Marie shrugged. 'But if they don't then it won't be for lack of trying.'

Now that I had chosen my path forward I was determined to do as good a job as I possibly could. Marie and her colleagues were being so good I wanted to help them in every way, so that they wouldn't end up wasting their time. We went over and over the document until we'd got it as accurate as we thought we possibly could. Marie then took it away to try to persuade her bosses that it was worth prosecuting.

She came back a few days later with a broad grin on her

face. 'My guv'nor reckons we should go after your mother as well,' she announced gleefully.

'Really?' I was amazed. 'What for?'

'He reckons she knew exactly what was going on and we could get her for neglect.'

In the end, however, they decided that going after Mum would be too difficult and they would focus their attention on proving the case against Richard.

I was thrilled. For a short time it was a huge weight off my shoulders. I felt I was finally moving forward towards a happy ending. But then reality struck. The whole process was going to take a year to come to court, during which time Richard would know we were after him and would be doubling his efforts to find us in order to intimidate us into silence.

The police assured me that once he was arrested he would be held on remand and we would be safe. As it was, they let him straight back onto the streets.

'You promised me you would hold onto him,' I groaned when they told me.

'I'm sorry, Janey,' Marie said. 'It was decided that he

was on too much medication for them to be able to risk it. If something went wrong and he got ill in custody the whole case could fall to pieces and he could end up suing the police. We just couldn't take the risk.'

'But he'll come looking for me,' I pleaded. 'I would never have started this whole thing if you hadn't promised he would be put away.'

'We'll do everything we can to protect you,' she assured me, and I knew she meant it. But what could she do if Richard or my brothers decided to wait outside the local school and lift Emma for a few hours, just to show me that they still had the power to do it? What would they do if the phone calls started coming in the middle of the night, or the notes came through the letterbox? What would they do if our house mysteriously caught fire in the night or Steve's car was run off the road on the way to work?

Although I didn't regret going to the police, I wasn't sure how I was going to get through the coming months of looking over my shoulder and jumping every time I heard a car pulling up outside the house or the telephone rang or Emma was a few minutes late coming out of school.

Once inside the house I hardly ever left, apart from taking the children across the road to school, and even then I didn't always make it, having to ask Steve or a friend to take them for me. It was as if my brain was too exhausted to cope. Every little thing Emma or Sophie asked for seemed as hard as climbing Mount Everest. If they wanted a drink I could barely summon the energy to find a beaker and fill it up.

Ideas of killing myself kept on coming to me and I wrote a long letter insisting that if I died the girls should both stay with Steve. My worst nightmare would be for Emma to be taken away and given back to my mother. I also wanted to make sure it was in writing that I didn't want Richard or Mum or my brothers coming to my funeral.

Every evening, after a hard day at the office, Steve would have to sit and listen to me drunkenly droning on about killing myself. In the end he lost patience.

'If you're going to do it there's nothing I can do about it,' he said one night. 'Just do it and get it over with. I'm going to bed.'

He went upstairs, leaving me snivelling in the lounge.

'Okay,' I thought, 'if I am going to do it then there are a few things I need to sort out.'

I had never got round to explaining to Emma about Paul being her real dad. Steve had been doing such a great job and she was so happy with him it hadn't seemed to be worth muddling things in her mind. But I didn't want to leave any unfinished business. It had been five years now since we had escaped. Emma was eight and old enough to understand. I sat her down at the kitchen table after school one day and explained it all to her. She listened with rapt attention, asked a few questions and seemed completely cool with the whole thing. I thought I should make contact with Paul and reintroduce him to his daughter before I got round to topping myself.

If I was going to make contact, however, I was also going to have to give him the full story of why we had to leave and all the things that had been going on behind his back when we were living together. I knew from the one or two people that we had managed to talk to in the old area that he had got engaged and that Emma now had a half-brother. I wanted Paul to meet her again and to think about introducing her to his other child, but I didn't know how to contact him.

Then Steve went for a lads' night out and bumped into a bloke he used to go to school with who played football with Paul. When he found out they still played, he asked if he would give Paul his number. The bloke assured him he would and we waited for the call. When it didn't come I was surprised, because I'd been sure Paul would call straightaway. Eventually the call did come and he told us the mutual friend had forgotten to give him the number. We met up and I told him the whole story. He was just as revolted and horrified as Steve had been, but I could almost see the pieces fitting into place in his head as he took my words in.

'So all those times when I came home early and the chain was on the door…' he said and I nodded, feeling sickened all over again to think of the things I was being forced to do every day of my life until we escaped.

Paul couldn't have been more understanding or more supportive. He promised to do everything he could to help me in the trial.

Now that I was finding my courage, I made contact with my dad and my baby brother Jimmy as well. Dad was happily remarried and had a successful painting and decorating firm which gave him a comfortable life. We started to visit him, but always had to keep ourselves hidden if anyone else from his family came round in case word got back that we were in the area. My mum's brother lived just over the road.

Dad was still living in blissful ignorance of the hell that I had been forced to live through after he left me. When I told him some of it I could see that he could hardly bear to listen, so I held back most of the details. It was then that he told me about how he used to get the dinner ladies at school to report back to him about how I was.

Even when I had explained everything to him he didn't seem to be able to take it all in. 'I can understand how he could do those things to you as a child,' he said one day, 'but how could you let him go on abusing you once you were a grown up with a baby of your own?'

I didn't feel it was my responsibility to enlighten him any further. Perhaps it would have been kinder to have left him to live out his life in blissful ignorance about the whole thing anyway. He shook his head in disbelief when I told him some of the things Mum had done too.

'She must have changed so much, Janey,' he said. 'I would never have married a woman like the one you're describing.'

Meeting Jimmy again after so many years was a shock. I don't know what I had expected, but it wasn't what I found. Jimmy's life experience since we had been parted couldn't have been more different from mine. He had been adopted by some kind people who had enough money to indulge his every whim. He was their only child and seemed to have no problems in his life, but still he wasn't happy and was having difficulty adapting to adulthood. I found I had little patience with him, and Steve had even less. It was disappointing after I had been carrying his memory around in my heart for so many years. Perhaps I was hoping that we would still be soulmates, as we had been when we were tiny and as we had remained in my mind all the years since. Maybe Jimmy was so damaged by his early years that no amount of love and security could overcome it, or maybe there was a genetic inheritance that he just couldn't shake off. Yet despite all that has happened over the years and the different paths that we have followed, I still love the man who was once the little boy I was forced to leave behind at the foster home and used to talk to through the birthmark on my arm.

Although in some ways my life was getting better, the black clouds of depression that I had always feared would arrive one day were growing darker all the time. I was constantly thinking about how much better off everyone would be without me, especially Steve and the girls. I was always miserable and felt I was no use to them at all.

I was continuing to buy drink and tablets, getting ready to make myself do something that I didn't really want to do. Eventually, having sat alone in the kitchen one morning screaming and crying, I drank enough to pluck up the courage to swallow a handful of powerful tranquillizers and anti-depressants. I'd already made arrangements for someone else to pick up the kids after school and keep them at their house until I came for them, believing I would be dead by then.

I don't think I can have taken enough tablets, though, because I was still able to walk to the front door when someone refused to stop banging on it.

'What have you done?' my friend asked when I opened the door and she saw the state of me.

I crumpled onto the floor in the kitchen, crawling into a corner and bawling my eyes out, just wanting it all to be over. I couldn't make my legs work any more. Every time I stood up, I fell down again. My friend went mad at me, shouting and screaming, and knowing what I had done because I'd been talking about it for so long. She called her mum, who was a nurse and lived just across the road, and the pair of them were shouting questions at me: 'How many have you taken?'

I tried to reply, but I wasn't making any sense, my words too slurred and my face numb.

My friend rang her husband, who came home from work and drove me up to the hospital. Once I got there I felt like a fool. I couldn't have taken enough tablets at all because they didn't even pump my stomach out, but they wouldn't let me go until they'd done some tests. I just wanted to sleep, I was so tired, but they wouldn't let me.

Steve came in later and wasn't pleased. 'I've had enough of this,' he said. 'I'm taking you home.'

After this I realized I was going to have to get a real grip if I was going to beat my demons and be a decent mother to the girls.

One of my main tasks in the year until the case came to court was to find as many witnesses as possible who would come forward and support my story. I needed people to testify how violent and frightening Richard was and how easily he would have been able to intimidate and bully a child into doing as he wanted. In my naiveté I thought that once they saw that I wasn't afraid to stand up to him, all the other members of the family would feel able to speak up too. He had beaten up, attacked and intimidated them over the years, so I actually thought they would be grateful to me for finally exposing him for the vicious, idle, cruel bully that he was. I remembered all the times Mum and the boys had said how much better life would be without him. Mum had always believed the boys would be the ones to save her from him when they were grown up, but maybe I would have to be the one to do it.

Unfortunately, I had underestimated Richard's powers to intimidate. One or two of my girlfriends from the past took my calls and agreed to be witnesses for me, but all of them rang back after talking to their husbands and partners to withdraw their support. No one, it seemed, wanted to put their lives, their homes and their families at risk. It appeared that Richard had succeeded yet again in making an entire community too terrified to stand up to him, even when they were offered the chance, but I completely understood how they felt. Hadn't he been able to keep me silent for twenty years?

There were also people I deliberately didn't approach because I knew they were too vulnerable. I knew they would do it for me, but Richard would kill them. Cheryl, for instance, had done a lot to help me over the years and I couldn't ask her to put herself in any more danger on my behalf.

I hadn't seen Hayley for so long I was very hesitant to contact her now and ask such a big favour, but eventually I could see that I needed all the help I could get.

'Of course I'll help you,' she said as soon as I asked, and I remembered how we had become blood sisters that day all those years ago. 'You should have asked me ages ago,' she went on. 'Your mum has already been round asking my mum to be a witness for them.'

'What did your mum say?'

'She said no, but their solicitors keep knocking on the door.'

It was wonderful to find that there were some people who had found the strength to stand up for what they believed to be right.

The more I found out, the more my head was spinning. I was shocked by how many of the older neighbours said that they had always known what was going on between Richard and me, as if it was inevitable and there was nothing they could have done about it. Maybe there *was* nothing they could have done, but at least they could have tried. Perhaps they assumed I was a willing participant in the relationship. Was that really possible?

Uncle John, who had been my friend in the days when he lived next door to us, also agreed to stand up and speak out against Richard.

'I know your granddad would never forgive me if I didn't help you when I had the chance,' he said. He would pay a terrible price later, branded a traitor to the family for siding with me against the precious patriarch.

Another of my uncles, who I knew had been beaten and bullied by Richard in the past, rang to tell me that Richard had asked him to be a witness for the defence and that he couldn't get out of it. I checked with Marie and she assured me that he would be perfectly within his rights to say no. I rang him back and told him he didn't have to do what Richard asked.

'But you know, Janey,' he whinged, 'I used to go down the pub with him sometimes. He's really just an ordinary bloke.'

As far as I knew Richard hardly ever went to the pub. The one occasion when he did go with this uncle he rolled back home blind drunk, having picked a fight on the way home then fallen over and dropped his Chinese all over the front garden. I think he knew that he couldn't handle his drink, which was why most of the time he and Mum just drank endless cups of tea.

'How can you be talking to me like that about a man who raped and abused me almost every day of my life for seventeen years?' I demanded.

'Oh, now hang on there, Janey,' my uncle cautioned, as if he was some wise elder of the family. 'We don't know that for sure. Everyone's innocent until they're proven guilty.'

'Why would I make stuff like that up?' I yelled, beside myself with fury that I was hearing this from a man who had himself suffered at Richard's hands. 'How could I imagine seventeen years of terror and pain?'

In the end they nearly all caved in except Hayley, Uncle John, Paul and Steve. I asked my dad if he would be at the court and he promised me he would. Steve's dad and two friends sat in for moral support.

Now that I was talking openly with so many people about what had happened in the past, things were beginning to click into place in my head and I was starting to feel better.

By now Steve was doing really well at work and had managed to buy us a better home in a nicer area which was even further from where my family was rooted. He had done brilliantly to earn enough to get a bigger mortgage and afford a nice house on a pleasant estate. The house was modern and nothing like the places I had lived in as a child. I should have felt that I was finally escaping my past. But I still found it impossible to enjoy anything good that happened to us. For so many years I had been conditioned to think that if something nice happened you would have to pay a penalty, do someone a favour or take a beating that I couldn't now believe it was possible our lives might be getting better.

As the first day of the case loomed closer I became increasingly nervous. What if no one believed me and the jury let Richard off? What if the men in the jury were doing the same things to their children that he had done to me? What if the judge did those sorts of things, or the barristers? What if I had to live the rest of my life in fear of Richard coming back for revenge? What if I was never able to get any sort of acknowledgement of what he had put me through? What if his bullying tactics proved to be successful in the end? How would I live with any of that?

Chapter Eleven

On the morning of the trial we saw the girls off to school before setting out for the court, trying to pretend that it was a normal day, but I doubt if we fooled them. They must have been able to sense the tension in the air.

We'd arranged to meet Marie and her colleagues from the police in the car park behind the court building, so they could let us in through a back entrance.

'They'll be waiting for you at the front entrance, trying to intimidate you,' Marie explained. 'We don't want you to have to meet up with them.'

Ushered quickly into the building, we were taken upstairs to a room that was set aside for witnesses waiting their turn in the box. None of us were allowed to talk to one another, even though Steve and I had been in a car together until a few minutes before. There were armchairs and we just had to sit and wait until we were called. There was no sign of my dad.

Nothing happened for hours, while the jury was being sworn in and other rituals that we knew nothing about were being gone through. We had assumed that they would call Steve first. He was looking forward to taking the stand. Richard had put him through a lot over the years and he relished the idea of putting things right at last.

'Jane Elliott,' an official called out. My heart lurched. I was going in first! I didn't want to leave the room full of friendly, supportive faces, knowing that Silly Git was going to be waiting for me in the courtroom and that there were going to be people trying to prove I was a liar and making me talk about things I didn't even want to think about any more. I walked out in a trance.

As I made my way into the courtroom one of my uncles and my brother Pete, whom I had more or less brought up as a little boy, were sitting by the door with their arms folded, just staring menacingly, trying to intimidate me, hoping to make me back down like every other person who had ever tried to put a stop to Silly Git's reign of terror. That was the first time I noticed that my brother had a tattoo on his neck, just like his dad.

'Don't look at them,' my officer instructed, trying to move me forward quickly. 'Don't look at them, they're just trying to unnerve you.'

I was shaking with fear, but I stared back at them as if I didn't care. The tension had been building towards this moment for a year, never mind the twenty or more years before that. I wasn't going to back down now. I had no respect for any of the people who had caved in and refused to back me up. After all he'd done to them as well. I stared back defiantly at my brother and uncle and shook my head, as if telling them that I couldn't believe what they were doing, that I was disappointed in them as men. I have no way of knowing whether they felt any shame or whether they had grown so used to obeying Richard that they actually believed it was right and normal. It certainly seemed he had been very successful in his campaign to convince them that 'families must stick together no matter what'.

Once I was inside the courtroom I bent my head to let my hair fall forward across my eyes, curtaining out everything except what was directly in front of me. I didn't want to see Silly Git's face if I could help it. I didn't want to imprint it afresh on my mind. I'd managed to put my memories into places where I could cope with them most of the time, I didn't want any fresh images to haunt me in the small hours of the morning.

To my relief I realized that as long as I kept the hair falling forward, he was going to be sitting outside my line of vision. I knew two of my friends were in the gallery, but I couldn't see them either.

My first day in the witness box was hard, as my barrister went over my childhood in every embarrassing detail. Everything had to be spelled out graphically, so that there could be no danger of any misunderstanding on the part of the judge or the jury and so that it could all be put down on the record. It was no good me referring coyly to 'his thing' if I meant 'his penis'. Every sex act had to be described without any modesty. There was nowhere for me to hide.

Although I was embarrassed to be talking about such things in front of strangers, I knew that my barrister was doing the right thing. He'd told the police that he had never worked on any case before where he was so determined to get justice for his client and to ensure that the defendant was imprisoned for as long as possible.

I noticed that Richard's defence lawyer was a striking-looking young black woman. She reminded me of the disco diva Grace Jones. I knew Richard wouldn't like that, holding the racist views that he did. And the chances were that he would have made his views known to her.

All the time I was giving evidence I kept my hair down, screening out his face, and that also helped to cover my embarrassment a little. I didn't want to see people pitying me in case I wasn't able to keep control of my voice. I was determined not to choke up, to ensure that I did the job as well as I possibly could. Every so often Silly Git would let out a rasping warning cough to let me know that even if I couldn't see him through my veil of hair he was just feet away from me, reminding me of all the threats he had made to me over the years about what would happen if I ever dared to tell anyone about our secrets, trying to bring me back down to the little girl he had pinned against the wall with a carving knife to her throat. He must have been able to see what agony I was in on that stand and he would have known he could have put a stop to it at any second if he had just decided he had done enough to me and had stood up and admitted it all. This was his one last chance to do something decent for the little girl he had taken responsibility for all those years ago, but he said nothing.

All I could see past my hair was the judge and one man sitting at the end of the jury. The juryman looked about forty years old and was wearing a leather jacket. As I told my story, he put his head in his hands several times and wept. I averted my eyes to cut the image out and just kept answering the questions. I felt bad for upsetting him.

I was dreading the time when my barrister would have asked all the questions he wanted to ask and it would be the turn of the opposition. Finally the moment came and Richard's lawyer stood up to confront me, her aim to prove that I was lying and had made the whole story up.

In all the courtroom dramas I had ever seen the opposing lawyers always managed to twist things to mean something different, making witnesses appear other than they were. But as the case continued, nothing this woman asked me seemed to be difficult to answer. All her questions just required honest replies and when I gave them she seemed to have nothing further to say. Once or twice she actually seemed to make things worse for her client by asking me about events that my own barrister hadn't thought to mention, all of which made Richard look and sound even more evil.

At one stage she asked me about his racial views, with regard to my status in the family as the 'Paki slave', and I had to tell her that he hated everyone of any other race and had tried to teach us to do the same. She asked if I had any racist opinions and I could honestly answer that I didn't.

When I was finally allowed to leave the witness box I noticed the floor was littered with a confetti of shredded paper from where I had been unknowingly plucking nervously at a ball of tissues.

At the end of my second day in the box, when I thought I had reached the end of my tether and could go no further, the judge apologized to me.

'I'm sorry, Jane,' he said, 'but I'm afraid you are going to have to come back again tomorrow.' My head dropped forward in a mixture of exhaustion and despair. 'I know, I know,' he went on as soothingly as he could. 'I'm sorry, but we do want this all cleared up, don't we?'

Having got this far I wasn't going to back out now.

My dad still hadn't made an appearance. I guess he thought it would be too hard to hear everything that had happened to his daughter being spelled out in detail.

The next day the judge stopped the proceedings and spoke to my barrister. 'I think we need to stop and change the direction of this case,' he said.

My heart sank. What did he mean?

'I don't think this is actually a case about child abuse,' he went on.

Not about child abuse? Then what were we all doing there? Hadn't he been listening to a single word of what I had been saying?

'I think,' he continued, 'it's about control and fear.'

'Yes!' I thought, my spirits soaring. At last the authorities understood what had been going on. That was what it had been about from the first day I came back from the foster home. It wasn't that Richard was just a paedophile, because he had continued his abuse long after I had turned into a woman; it was about something even more premeditated and cold-blooded than that. He had tried to steal my whole life, and had succeeded in getting away with seventeen years of it before I managed to stop him, although it could have been argued that he had stolen the following years as well by leaving me in such a vulnerable and unhappy state.

After a break in the proceedings I was being led back into the courtroom by a victim liaison officer, an elderly lady. Up till then they had been careful to take me in and out of a different door from Silly Git, or if they hadn't then they had made sure we didn't meet, which was making me feel more confident. Hiding behind my hair, I had still been able to avoid seeing him and remembering his face too clearly. As I came back in through the door with my head down I saw a pair of shoes directly ahead of me, blocking my way. I looked up, straight into a face that made me feel sick with fear. The pale snakelike eyes and the ginger hair were the same, although he looked a little stockier than I remembered him.

'Get me out of here,' I hissed through gritted teeth, feeling his eyes boring into mine and his thoughts getting back inside my head. 'Get me out, get me out.'

'Calm down, for heaven's sake,' the lady said, irritated by such a show of emotion. 'Come through here.'

She led me into a room off the court, which had a glass door. He followed us, but didn't come in, standing outside the glass, just staring at me with no expression.

'Get the police!' I screamed. 'Get the police!'

'Don't be silly, dear,' she was losing patience now. 'Who is it you're worried about? Is it him?' She gestured towards the immobile figure on the other side of the glass with the dead, staring eyes.

'Get someone!' I screamed and she realized there was no way she could calm me down. She walked towards the door. 'Don't leave me!' I screamed, suddenly envisaging him and me in the room alone. The woman was panicking now, aware that she didn't know how to handle the situation.

At that moment Marie and another police officer arrived. Finding me standing in the corner of the room, hiding my face against the wall like a child in trouble, they came to the rescue, furious with everyone and getting me to safety.

'He's going to kill me,' I moaned as Marie put her arm round me. 'I'm dead.'

'No, he won't, Jane,' she soothed me. 'He can't do anything now. You're doing fine. It's nearly over.'

I wanted to be in the courtroom to hear Richard's testimony once I had said all I had to say. He had been willing to sit there and listen to me as I squirmed with embarrassment relating every detail of my humiliation through the years, so it seemed only fair that I should witness his humiliation.

'We can't stop you coming in,' Marie said, 'but we really don't think it would be a good idea. They're going to tell all sorts of lies to try to make you look bad and to make out that you are a liar and a fantasist. You'll find it very hard to listen to.'

I took her advice. I'd already had a taste of the sort of things my stepfather's barrister had been briefed to try to pin on me. She had tried to imply that I was a regular drug user and that my flats were always full of men, both of which were accusations I could easily dismiss. I might have had the odd puff of pot in my time, but the thought of experimenting with anything harder when you already have a head full of demons like mine would be too terrifying to contemplate.

They had also tried to claim that my welfare had been monitored by social services, but my barrister had made that claim look foolish. They had suggested that I was paranoid, believing that everyone and everything was against me, and that I was an attention-seeker, but the judge and jury didn't seem impressed by any of that either. The worst thing they said was that if I had been interfered with, then it would have been my granddad who had done it, not my stepdad.

Over the next few days I heard odd snippets about what was happening in the courtroom. Steve, Paul, Uncle John and Hayley all did their bits, while everyone else in the family came forward to swear blind that

Richard had never hit them and that he was a sweet, gentle man, just an ordinary bloke.

Apparently at one point in the proceedings my brother Pete took exception to something my barrister said and jumped over the barrier to try to take a swing at him. Years of training in the boxing ring, coupled with the philosophy that violence was always the answer to everything, were now working against my family. The more they postured and threatened and swaggered, the more they confirmed the way they were.

Finally it was over. We had said all that we had to say and it was up to the jury to decide whether or not I was telling the truth. If they thought that I was, then the judge would have to decide what to do about it.

I couldn't even guess what the outcome might be. By now I'd lost track of whether what had happened to me was extraordinary or not. The reaction of everyone who heard my story suggested that it was unusual and shocking, but then my family made it appear that such behaviour was normal, that nothing that had happened to me merited anyone being punished. I no longer knew what to think about anything.

One of the things I was saddest about was that my family now knew about Sophie. I had managed to keep her existence secret from them, but now they knew I had two daughters when I didn't want them to know anything about my new life.

The jury stayed out for a long time and Marie and my barrister told me that was good, but I really wanted to get it all over with and to know what would be happening next. Everyone told me that they had good vibes and that they were sure we were going to win, but I kept thinking, 'What if we don't? What if they find him not guilty on any of the charges and he's free to leave the court? What would I feel like then? And once he was free, what would he do to exact his revenge on me for telling the world the truth about him?'

Steve and I went to a pub close to the courthouse to wait. We wanted to be with the people who had stood up for me in the court. I wanted to share the result with them because they were the ones who had stuck by me through the whole thing, refusing to be intimidated into silence or lies like all the others. My dad turned up for the last day as well. It was one of those big pubs where you can sit around all day on sofas ordering coffees and drinks and snacks. We got there early in the morning, not wanting to miss the announcement, and the hours ticked slowly by.

Every so often my mobile would ring, making my heart miss a beat, but it would just be Marie, telling us that there was no news but not to worry, that they had all gone to lunch or that they were all back from lunch. Hour after hour we talked over everything that had happened in the courtroom and debated every facial expression that the jury or the judge had shown.

'I caught that judge's eye, you know,' Steve's dad kept saying, 'and he gave me a look which just said, "I know, mate. I know."'

All the signs seemed good, but how often do you read about cases where the verdict is completely the opposite to what everyone expects? How was I to know what influence Richard had exerted on the jury? Could he have intimidated them like he did everyone else? I forced all the negative thoughts from my mind.

At about three o'clock the phone went again, making me jump.

'It's Marie. The result is in.'

'Yeah?' I hardly dared breathe.

'He's been found guilty of all the charges except one, which he got off on a technicality.'

'Guilty? So how long will be get?'

'They won't do the sentencing for a few weeks,' she said. 'But the judge did warn him that he would be going away for a very long time.'

'Does that mean they'll be letting him out until the sentencing?' I felt a lurch of panic in my stomach.

'No,' Marie laughed. 'He'll be on remand. He won't be going anywhere for a very long time.'

Chapter Twelve

When Marie rang a few weeks later to tell me that Richard had been given fifteen years, the maximum sentence that a judge could give for the crimes he had been found guilty of, I felt a little pang of disappointment.

'But that's really good, Jane,' Marie assured me.

'I know,' I said, 'it's just that he took seventeen years of my life, and well, you know…'

Once I had got used to the idea, however, I was pleased, and very grateful to everyone who had helped me do it.

'Just think, Mummy,' Emma said to me the evening after the sentencing, 'we're going up to our own beds now and that horrible man has got to go to sleep in a cold cell. Serves him right for what he did to you.'

The girls know that I had a cruel stepfather who did things to me that you shouldn't do to children, but they don't yet know the extent of it. Emma can remember the occasional time when Silly Git had me pinned against the wall by the throat, but I don't think it worries her because she knows that my story has a happy ending.

The outcome of the case wasn't happy for everyone. My brothers went after the people who had stood up for me. One of them chased Hayley in her car, eventually forcing her to stop. He ran over to her, kicking at the car to try to get her out so he could get at her and shouting how he was going to kill her. She went to the police but the rest of the family gave him an alibi, saying he was with them at the time she alleged the incident happened. Her family started getting threatening phone calls all night long as well.

My Uncle John also started receiving threatening calls. He was attacked beside the grave at a family funeral as punishment for 'betraying the family' and his car was sprayed with obscenities. It was his brother's funeral, the uncle who had tried to intimidate me as I went into court, who had died soon afterwards from the family complaint of kidney failure. The fight at the graveside escalated when Uncle John's wife tried to help and got her face slapped for her trouble.

Paul had the windows of his house and his car smashed and Steve's mum and dad started receiving threats on their lives, notes through the door and phone calls telling them what was going to happen to them, and people sitting outside their house in cars, with the headlights shining through the windows, beeping incessantly on the horns. The police gave us, Steve's parents and Hayley's family all alarms in our houses as well as mobile ones to carry around, which we can keep for the rest of our lives. Paul has now joined the police force and had a second son. I'm very proud of him for making something good of his life.

I kept hoping that once Richard had been inside for a while and they had all had a chance to think about things, they would realize that I had done them an enormous favour in rescuing them from a man who had been bullying them all for more than twenty years. I couldn't understand why it was taking them so long to realize. I presumed they must all still be frightened of him, even though he was inside.

A month or two before the sentencing Steve's parents had received a call from my brother Tom. 'Please don't put the phone down,' he said. 'I don't have anything to do with that lot and I desperately need to speak to Janey because I can't believe all this stuff has been happening.'

'Give us your number,' they said. 'We'll pass it on to Janey and she can call you if she wants.'

I had been wanting to get in touch with Tom for years, fearing that he might be the one Richard would pick on once he didn't have me to kick around. He and Dan had always been my favourites. When he was a baby and I was trying to get him to sleep, I used to suck on his ear lobes so much that I ended up stretching them and making them floppy. He was the one I'd thought about rescuing when we first escaped from the area. I'd heard through friends of Steve's that he had been beaten up badly and chased out of the house and had been living on the streets and getting into drugs.

I had an old pay-as-you-go mobile which wouldn't be traceable, so I passed that number to him.

'Don't you live with them, then?' I asked when he called.

'No,' he said. 'I've only just found out about the court case because I bumped into Dan up the market.'

'Yeah?'

'But I ended up with two black eyes.'

'How come?'

'Well, Dan told me you weren't our real sister, but you are, aren't you?'

'No, I'm only your half-sister.'

'Oh.' He was quiet for a moment. 'Well, I called him a liar and he was saying stuff about you and I wouldn't have it. I said we love each other.'

'Still got your wobbly ears then?'

'Yes.' He laughed at the memory.

I was very pleased to have got in touch with him again.

After the sentencing had been announced the local papers asked if they could report it. I was happy to agree. I knew how helpful it had been to me to read *A Child Called It*. If just one child read an article about me and realized that they too could do something about what was being done to them then it would be worthwhile.

A journalist was sent to interview me and at the moment she arrived at the house the mobile phone

I had used to talk to Tom went off. Somehow the rest of the family had got hold of the number and now they were all screaming down the phone at me, telling me on the one hand I'd torn the family apart, that I'd taken away someone they loved and that they were going to do the same to me, and on the other hand that I had brought them all together for the first time in years. It seemed that family members who hadn't spoken to one another for ages had suddenly come together to confront the common enemy: me.

'We know where Steve works,' one of them was yelling. 'We're gonna fucking kill him. We know where his parents live, they're gonna end up fucking burned alive in their beds.'

Buoyed up by the successful verdict, I was giving as good as I got, screaming that they should be grateful that I'd put Richard away and that he wouldn't be able to hurt any of them any more, but none of them were having it. Families, apparently, should stick together and protect their own, even when their own have been proven to be monsters.

A woman I'd never met came on the line, hurling abuse at me for taking away her kids' grandfather. She was married to one of my brothers and would still have been a kid herself at the time I left home.

'I'm gonna beat the fucking shit out you!' she screamed. 'Do you know who I am? I'm well 'ard. And we know where you live.'

'Alright then, if you know where I live, I'm on the doorstep, come and get me. Don't forget I know where you live too,' I said, naming the street.

Some other bloke I had never met in my life then came on telling me how he was going to cut me open.

'You don't even know me!' I said.

'We know where your husband works, so tell him to keep checking the brakes on his car.'

Then Silly Git's sister came on the line and was trying to convince me that the boys were heartbroken at losing their father.

'So do you think I should have let him get away with it then?' I asked.

'All I'm saying is that I've just had to run round the block with your brother who's being chased with a knife because of this.'

'That's it,' I thought, 'this lot are loving it. They're

never happier than when they're winding someone up. Any day without a good fight story to tell is a wasted day to them.'

In the background I heard my mother's voice shouting over the rest. 'What's the matter with her then? Is she missing his cock?'

I hung up the phone. There was nothing left to say really.

The poor little journalist couldn't get out of the house quick enough.

Now it's all over and Steve and I can concentrate on bringing up the girls in a normal family atmosphere. I feel I've done what I had to. Now I'm Mrs Elliott, a normal wife and mum, taking my children back and forth to school, running the home and walking the dog, but there will always be a hole where my past should have been.

Some old schoolfriends contacted me through the Internet and invited me to a reunion in a pub near the old school. I wanted to see them all, but it was hard to travel back to the area where my family still lived. In the end I summoned all my courage – after all, Silly Git had been taken off the street and I reckoned I could deal with my brothers. I used to change their nappies, for God's sake!

'Oh my God!' the girls shrieked when they saw me coming into the reunion. 'It's the nutter herself.'

I gave a joyful laugh at the sight of all their familiar faces.

'Ah, you've still got that terrible laugh!' they cried.

As we got talking they started to tease me about my accent. 'You've started putting "t"s in the middle of words like water,' they laughed. 'You're getting posh.'

'That's funny,' I laughed, 'because where I live now they think I'm dead common.'

When I finally decided to write this book and I told the children, Emma wanted to know why I wasn't going to use our real names.

'Well,' I took a deep breath, 'there may be people at school who will read about the horrible things that happened to me when I was young and will tease you about it, and I wouldn't want that.'

'Well, I would just tell them to shut up,' she said, with a look of puzzlement, 'and I would tell them my mum was really brave and I was really proud of you.'

Epilogue

Once Richard was behind bars I started to become more confident about going back to the area where the family used to live to visit a friend or go out. I always travelled with someone else and stressed that no one should tell anyone in my family that I was there, but I was beginning to feel safer. Even so, I was always anxious not to push my luck. Although things had gone well at the school reunion I'd attended, when I was told about another one I was reluctant to go. It seemed to me that I was tempting fate to go back for such a public event.

Several friends, however, who had found me through Friends Reunited, were bombarding me with e-mails saying that I had to come. The girls were telling me that everyone was going to be there and they all really wanted to see me, and the blokes told me not to worry because they wouldn't let anything happen to me. It felt really nice to think that they all wanted to see me so much and since Steve was going to be away on business for a few nights anyway, I decided to take my courage in both hands and go.

I booked a train ticket and took a taxi to Tanya's house. The plan was for us to meet at a pub and then go on to a club afterwards. It was a sunny summer's evening and although I was nervous about being back in the area, I was looking forward to a good night out.

As we got out of the car outside the pub I saw a group of our friends already sitting at one of the tables and at the same moment I spotted some of my cousins coming out of the pub with drinks. One of them was Tracy, the girl that Silly Git had made me fight with all those years ago.

'Janey!' the table of old schoolfriends shouted at the tops of their voices. 'Over here, Janey!'

The moment I saw the expressions on my cousins' faces I knew that I was in danger. I remembered the phone call with all of them screaming abuse and telling me how I'd managed to unite the whole family against me and I realized I had made a terrible mistake. They were already reaching for their phones. I went straight up to the table of friends and spoke to Al, a big guy who works as a club bouncer.

'You've got to get me out of here now, Al. Get the police over here.'

'What?' he looked puzzled.

There was a police station right next door to the pub. It would only have taken a few seconds to get someone over.

'Calm down, Janey,' Al said. 'You're quite safe here.'

I could see that I wasn't going to be able to convince him and I didn't think I had much time to spare. I ran into the pub, already breathless with panic. If I could get into the kitchens maybe I could find a back way out.

'I'm sorry, you can't go in there, that's the kitchen.' A girl barred my way.

'You've got to help me!' I was shouting. 'You've got to get me out of here and call the police! They're gonna kill me!'

She obviously thought I was mad and there was no way she was letting me through those doors. Tanya and Al were with me now and were beginning to catch on to the urgency of the situation, while trying to calm me down at the same time.

The girl showed us to a room and said she would go and talk to her manager.

'Lock us in and call the police!' I shouted at her, but the more hysterical I became, the less seriously I could see she was taking me. I would have dialled the police myself, but my hands were shaking too much to even hold a phone.

The girl was back a few moments later. 'My manager says you have to leave,' she said. 'You can go out through the back door to the alley and round to the street.'

'I can't go round to the street, that's where they are!' I shouted, but she was already ushering us out into the alley amongst the bins. I could see the police station from there and in a church next door a couple were getting married. It all looked so normal, but such a long way away.

'Let me wait here a second,' I pleaded.

'I'm afraid my manager says I have to shut the door,' the girl said and I saw it closing as if in slow motion.

'Nooooo!' I screamed as the lock clicked and I heard the screech of tyres in the road.

'Oh my God, they're here!' Tanya shrieked and I saw a gang of six men coming up the alley towards us. The one at the front was brandishing a broom handle. They all looked familiar, but in my confusion I couldn't work out who was who. Later I was told that the man with the broom handle was my brother Tom, the one who had told me that we loved each other. In my mind he was still a little boy, just like the others. I couldn't believe that my brothers had turned into this mob of men. They all looked like Richard as they poured into the tight little alley.

Al walked forward with his arms stretched out, trying to block their way, but they smacked him to the ground and just kept coming, trampling over his prone body. The one at the front picked me up by the arms and threw me to the ground. Tanya, who was running out into the street screaming for help, heard the crack of my skull hitting the pavement. For the next few moments everything was a blur as I drifted in and out of consciousness. The man they tell me was Tom was kicking my head and bringing the broom handle down with all the force that I remembered from my beatings as a child. As he hit and kicked, he shouted the same furious obscenities that I remembered coming from Richard's mouth so many times before. Another man was kicking my head from the other side. I could hear crunching inside my head. Others behind were kicking at my ribs and legs with all their strength. Through their legs I could see two men laying into Al as he lay on the ground.

'You're gonna kill her!' I heard one of the cousins shouting and they began to struggle with one another as some tried to pull others off me, but they kept on kicking.

One man I went to school with had responded to Tanya's shouts for help, but when he looked into the alley he changed his mind. 'Fucking hell!' he exclaimed. 'They're fucking nutters. I'm not getting mixed up in that.' Another guy from school did try to intervene, but was headbutted and on the ground in seconds.

By the time the police had made it across the street my family had finished and run away. I lay on the ground, unable to see or hear anything. I knew that I had wet myself. Someone had opened the door to the pub and they started pulling me back into the room. I couldn't stop myself from screaming and crying, terrified that they would make me go back out the front where I was sure my family would be waiting for me. The girl who had shut us out in the alley was almost as hysterical as I was, but I found it hard to be sympathetic, having begged her for help and received none. I was more concerned about who was waiting for me outside.

'Janey,' someone tried to reassure me, 'half the police force are out there now.'

Eventually they managed to calm me down enough to get me out to the waiting ambulance, but the first thing I saw was some of my cousins circling around on their mobile phones, reporting what was happening to the ones who had run away. There was also an abandoned car outside the police station, surrounded by policemen.

Later, I fitted the pieces of the jigsaw together. My attackers had arrived in such a hurry they had driven straight over the roundabout outside the police station and the police had been called out to deal with the dangerous driving before they had known anything about what was happening to me. When my attackers had run back to the car, leaving me for dead, they were unable to start it and had to scatter on foot, leaving the abandoned car with their mobile phones buzzing for the police to pick up the calls.

Later that night two of my brothers, realizing that their phones had given them away, turned themselves in to get their phones and car back.

As I was loaded into the ambulance I saw the wedding party groom on the steps of the church, trying to enjoy the day, and I felt so guilty. It seemed that it was all my fault that their day had been ruined. I was also afraid I'd ruined the school reunion, but I discovered later, as I was being X-rayed and patched up in hospital, that they had kept the party going and gone on to the club as planned. I felt terrible that Al had taken such a kicking on my behalf, but apparently he was able to keep going for the night.

I called my dad, hoping that he would come down to the hospital and give me some moral support, but it turned out he'd had a few drinks and couldn't drive. I rang Steve's parents and they were at the hospital by the time I arrived and sat with me throughout the night. The staff wanted me to stay in, but I wanted to get out of the area as soon as possible and back to the kids. I didn't want them to have to spend Sunday without either of their parents around.

For the next few days, whenever I looked in the mirror, I was reminded of all the times that I had seen my mother with her head swollen out of shape, her eyes closed up and the bruising coming through.

But despite everything I know I was right to speak out.

Hannah's Gift

MARIA HOUSDEN

Lessons from a life fully lived

During the last year of her short life, Maria Housden's three-year-old daughter Hannah was fearless in the way she faced death, and irrepressibly joyful in the way she approached living. The little girl who wore her favourite red shoes into the operating theatre changed the life of everyone who came into contact with her.

In a lyrically told narrative, both moving and unforgettable, Housden recounts Hannah's battle with cancer in simple, straightforward language that transcends grief and fear to become a celebration. From Hannah's story emerge five profound lessons – of truth, joy, faith, compassion and wonder – that have the power to change our lives. A remarkable story, remarkably told, it will bring comfort to anyone touched by loss, and renewed faith in the power of love.

> A heartbreaking and heartwarming tale of a fearless little girl. *People Magazine*

> Hannah has a philosophy on life that is unique and tears the heart apart. *The Bookseller*

Maria Housden is a lecturer, author and passionate advocate for quality of life at the end of life. The mother of three children in addition to Hannah, she and her husband Roger now live in Woodstock, New York.

One Child

TOREY HAYDEN

She was a wild, violent six-year-old lost in a world of anger and torment – until a brilliant young teacher reached out

Six-year-old Sheila was abandoned by her mother on a highway when she was four. A survivor of horrific abuse, she never spoke and never cried. She was placed in a class for severely retarded children after committing an atrocious act of violence against another child.

Everyone thought Sheila was beyond salvation – except her teacher, Torey Hayden. With patience, skill and abiding love, she fought long and hard to release a haunted little girl from her secret nightmare, and nurture the spark of genius she recognized was trapped within Sheila's silence. This is the remarkable story of their journey together – an odyssey of hope, courage and inspiring devotion that opened the heart and mind of one lost child to a new world of discovery and joy.

Page after page proves again the power of love and the resiliency of life. *Los Angeles Times*

Torey Hayden deserves the kind of respect I can't give many people. She isn't just valuable, she's incredible. The world needs more like Torey Hayden.

Boston Globe

Help Yourself

DAVE PELZER

How you can find hope, courage and happiness

Dave Pelzer willed himself to overcome the worst life had to offer (his case of child abuse was one of the worst recorded in US history) and became the best he could be. *Help Yourself* weaves in stories from Pelzer's own experiences with the principles he has discovered on how to survive difficulty and embrace challenges as an opportunity for growth. This inspiring conclusion to Dave Pelzer's bestselling autobiography takes Dave's story up to the present and shows us the way forward, for the first time offering readers the invaluable life lessons Dave learned along the way.

> What has made Dave Pelzer's story a bestseller is that it is a story of redemption. It is a story where love, kindness, patience and endurance triumph. *Daily Mail*

> Pelzer's unyielding determination inspires us all. He is a living example that all of us have the capability to better ourselves no matter what the odds.
> Jack Canfield, co-author of *Chicken Soup for the Soul*

Dave Pelzer is the internationally bestselling author of *A Child Called 'It'*, *The Lost Boy* and *A Man Named Dave*. He travels throughout the world raising awareness about child abuse and prevention and inspiring hope and resilience in thousands.

S P E C I A L O F F E R

Order these selected Thorsons and Element titles direct from the publisher and receive £1 off each title! Visit www.thorsonselement.com for additional special offers.

Free post and packaging for UK delivery (overseas and Ireland, £2.00 per book).

Hannah's Gift Maria Housden (ISBN 0-00-715567-0)	£6.99 - £1 = £5.99
Unravelled Maria Housden (ISBN 0-00-718063-2)	£5.99 - £1 = £4.99
Dave Pelzer's Life Lessons Dave Pelzer (ISBN 0-00-714691-4)	£4.99 - £1 = £3.99
One Child Torey Hayden (ISBN 0-00-719905-8)	£5.99 - £1 = £4.99

Place your order by post, phone, fax, or email, listed below. Be certain to quote reference code **714S** to take advantage of this special offer.

Mail Order Dept. (REF: **714S**)
HarperCollins*Publishers*
Westerhill Road
Bishopbriggs G64 2QT

Email: customerservices@harpercollins.co.uk
Phone: 0870 787 1724
Fax: 0870 787 1725

Credit cards and cheques are accepted. Do not send cash. Prices shown above were correct at time of press. Prices and availability are subject to change without notice.

BLOCK CAPITALS PLEASE

Name of cardholder ______________________
Address of cardholder ______________________
____
____

Postcode __________

Delivery address (if different)
____
____
____

Postcode __________

I've enclosed a cheque for £______, made payable to HarperCollins*Publishers*, or please charge my Visa/MasterCard/Switch (circle as appropriate)

Card Number: ______________________

Expires: __/__ Issue No: __/__ Start Date: __/__

Switch cards need an issue number or start date validation.

Signature: ______________________

thorsons element

Make

www.thorsonselement.com

your online sanctuary

www.thorsonselement.com

Get online information, inspiration and guidance to help you on the path to physical and spiritual well-being. Drawing on the integrity and vision of our authors and titles, and with health advice, articles, astrology, tarot, a meditation zone, author interviews and events listings, www.thorsonselement.com is a great alternative to help create space and peace in our lives.

So if you've always wondered about practising yoga, following an allergy-free diet, using the tarot or getting a life coach, we can point you in the right direction.